Primary Mathematics
for Teaching Assistants

Also available:

Primary Science for Teaching Assistants
Rosemary Feasey
1–84312–447–5

Primary ICT for Teaching Assistants
John Galloway
1–84312–446–7

ICT for Teaching Assistants
John Galloway
1–84312–203–0

Primary Mathematics for Teaching Assistants

Sylvia Edwards

Routledge
Taylor & Francis Group

LONDON AND NEW YORK

First published 2007
by Routledge
2 Park Square, Milton Park, Abingdon OX14 4RN

Simultaneously published in the USA and Canada
by Routledge
270 Madison Avenue, New York, NY 10016

Routledge is an imprint of the Taylor & Francis Group, an informa business

Typeset by RefineCatch Limited, Bungay, Suffolk
Printed and bound in Great Britain by Bell & Bain Ltd, Glasgow

British Library Cataloguing in Publication Data
A catalogue record for this book is available from the British Library

Library of Congress Cataloging in Publication Data
A catalog record for this book has been applied for.

ISBN10 1-84312-428-9 (pbk)

ISBN13 978-1-84312-428-3 (pbk)

Contents

v

Preface

How good are you at mathematics? Do you need help to support the teaching of mathematics in schools? Perhaps you are an aspiring Higher Level Teaching Assistant? If so, this book is for you! It is packed with practical advice and information for adults who support children's learning in mainstream and special schools.

This is not simply a book on how to do mathematics. It is about how to help as many children as possible to develop their mathematical potential. It focuses on the teaching of mathematics in Key Stages 1 and 2, reflecting the renewed Primary Framework (DfES 2006), but staff in secondary schools may find it helpful for supporting secondary students who need to work from earlier Key Stages. The book also aims to help adults who may feel challenged by some of the mathematical language and concepts taught in schools to develop confidence and feel more able to support pupils independently.

What does the book do? The first chapter clarifies the notion of mathematics and its application to adult life, outlining some principles of successful teaching and learning. Subsequent chapters explore the developmental sequence of mathematics in primary schools and offer strategies and resources to support the core objectives. Chapter 7 includes strategies for pupils' self-assessment and involvement in their progress. The book concludes with ideas for using interactive resources to support mathematical development and enhance motivation.

This handbook will help develop your understanding of pupils' learning experiences and expectations in mathematics and enhance your ability to promote success for the learners you support.

Mathematics – what do we mean?

Being numerate involves understanding the number system and its methods of computation: addition, subtraction, multiplication and division. Numeracy is also about the concepts that give meaning to numbers, such as fractions, decimals, percentages or ratio. Mathematics is a broader application of the number system. It includes solving problems to do with the concepts of shape and space, time, weight and mass, capacity and money, as well as understanding numerical data.

The National Numeracy Framework describes numeracy as:

a proficiency which involves confidence and competence with numbers and measures . . . an understanding of the number system, a repertoire of computational skills and an inclination and an ability to solve number problems in a variety of contexts . . . practical understanding of the ways in which information is gathered by counting and measuring and is presented in graphs, charts and tables. (DfEE 1999b:4)

How numerate are you?

How numerate or mathematical do you consider yourself? You probably know far more about mathematics than you realise. Think about some of the mathematical problems you have dealt with at work or at home. At the time of writing, I have:

- put fuel in my car
- calculated how much deposit I've paid for a holiday and how much the remaining balance is, with insurance
- bought numerous items at the local shop and at the supermarket
- worked out a reduction of 20 per cent on a coat in a sale
- looked at the *TV Times* to see what programmes were on
- shortened some curtains
- reduced ingredients for spaghetti bolognese, for two people instead of four
- checked my bank statement
- bought my lunches during the week
- worked out meeting times for my job, allowing sufficient travelling time
- studied data on pupil progress, presented as a range of graphs.

This list is only part of the mathematics I do – we all do a huge amount, every day. Think about some of the skills and knowledge I needed to do the above tasks.

To work out my holiday balance, I had to *subtract* the deposit from the total amount. Then to pay the holiday insurance, I *multiplied* the amount per person by 2. I then *added* both amounts together. To pay for my shopping I mentally *added* up what was in my basket as I went along, offered the correct notes and coins and checked my change by *subtracting* it from what I had given.

To calculate the reduction on that coat in the sale, I converted 20 per cent to one fifth (you might have done this differently), *divided* the total amount by 5 then *subtracted* the fifth from the original price. The curtains were too long so they had to be measured in centimetres. I then had to calculate how much to allow for the hem before cutting off the excess length. For the spaghetti bolognese, I needed to know that 2 is half of 4 and to halve the ingredients as I went along. Finally I had to consider my range of graphs and my travelling by car and by train.

Most of us do similar mathematical tasks every day, without even thinking about it. You will have noticed that all four methods of computation, addition, subtraction, multiplication and division, have featured in my snapshot of everyday mathematics, as has time, money, data and shape and space.

Mathematics is for life!

Mathematics does not exist in a vacuum. Numerical thinking and problem- solving are integral to our daily lives. 'Sums' are not delivered to us ready-packaged with instructions on whether to add, subtract, multiply or divide. The thinking and the problem-solving are part of the process. Life is the mathematical context!

Not all children can develop into high-level mathematicians. Some will need mathematics for use in their jobs. Others will mainly use mathematics at a basic level to go about their daily lives. Nevertheless, all children are entitled to receive learning opportunities through which they can develop mathematical understanding according to individual potential. Success partly depends on how mathematics is taught and nurtured in learners. But, at the end of schooling, mathematics is for life!

What is involved in learning mathematics?

Consider what is involved in mathematical thinking:

- facts – knowing formulas and tables (such as $2 \times 3 = 6$)
- understanding – in order to use the facts to solve problems
- knowledge – of a range of mathematical areas (for example, at a simple level, knowing that 6 is less than 9, or that 4 $\frac{1}{4}$s comprise a whole 1)
- relationships – between different facts and knowledge (for example, knowing that 0.2 is $\frac{1}{5}$)

- strategy and methods – for applying known facts and knowledge
- thinking – in order to problem-solve
- memory – in order to retain information long enough to problem-solve.

How might we help learners develop the attributes listed above? First, we need to promote positive attitudes. Mathematics is everywhere – not just in numeracy lessons. It's in the collection of data by the school office and money for dinners and sponsorships by classroom teachers, for instance. Both of these activities contribute to the perceptions that children cultivate about mathematics.

We can promote positive perceptions by:

- reinforcing mathematics in the playground (skipping games, throwing, etc.)
- role-playing trips to supermarket, bank or travel agent
- talking about mathematics that is relevant to children, for example, talking about children's birthdays to stimulate and support an understanding of time.

Try listing the range of mathematical thinking that children are involved with. Thinking around their pocket money is one example. By linking mathematics to everyday life, we will help children see learning in mathematics as essential.

Mathematics across the curriculum

All subjects contribute to children's perceptions of mathematics. Art media such as paintings, photographs and sculpture illustrate mathematical ideas of shape, form and symmetry. Practically, mixing quantities of paint involves multiplication and ratio. History compares past with present, requiring vocabulary related to time. In geography, children interpret maps and scales. All subjects present information in the form of tables, graphs and charts. Cross-curricular approaches help children to see mathematics as an extensive area of learning, the objective of which is to solve problems.

Mathematics and problem-solving

One reason why many children do not do as well as expected in the National Curriculum SAT assessments is because they are not able to translate problems into sums. Examples in Figures 1.1 to 1.4 illustrate the types of problems posed for Key Stage 1 pupils.

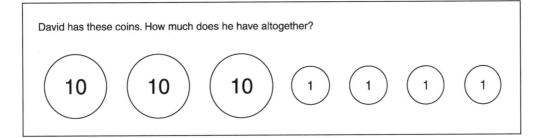

Figure 1.1 Money

David makes cakes with these:	Amy makes double the number of cakes.
1 egg	Write the missing numbers:
3 spoons of flour	2 eggs
2 spoons of sugar	_____ spoons of flour
2 spoons of milk	_____ spoons of sugar
	_____ spoons of milk

Figure 1.2   Doubling

Children made a chart of the fruits they liked best.	
Bananas	x x x x
Oranges	x x x x x x x
Apples	x x x
Peaches	x x x x x
Pears	x x
How many more children chose oranges than peaches?	

Figure 1.3   Understanding charts

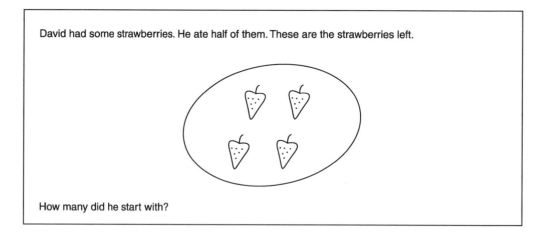

David had some strawberries. He ate half of them. These are the strawberries left.

How many did he start with?

Figure 1.4   Understanding half

What can we say about Figure 1.1? Most children count in 10s and 1s without difficulty, but this problem requires them to first count the 10p coins and then count the 1p coins, changing the *thought process* part way through the operation. Many children struggle to do this.

Figure 1.2 requires doubling of numbers to 10. This is a task that most children will have practised regularly, but many fail to see the problem as one of doubling because it is disguised within the context of baking.

Figure 1.3 illustrates a common misunderstanding – children usually associate the word 'more' with addition. The problem requires some addition, to add up the symbols matched to the oranges and peaches, but the question 'more . . . than' requires a subtraction.

Figure 1.4 is not what it seems. Children associate the word 'half' with sharing and division. This question asks them to work out how many strawberries David *started with* by doubling what he left.

These kinds of problems could be solved more easily with further practice.

A final thought – why are some people brilliant at mathematics while others struggle to understand it? Is success in mathematics the result of innate intelligence or good teaching? There is no simple answer to these questions, but by the end of this book we may find a response less elusive.

CHAPTER 2

Principles for success

This chapter outlines some principles for teaching and learning that might enable more children to become 'good' at mathematics.

Linking facts and methods with understanding

Dawn, in Year 6, often says she is 'stuck' in mathematics lessons because she cannot think what to do. Dawn relies on remembering taught methods because she often fails to understand the mathematical concepts. There are many children with similar difficulties who, having forgotten a particular method, cannot *think* their way through a problem because they don't understand it.

Many key mathematical facts are learned by rote, for example, multiplication tables, doubles of numbers and number bonds to 10. Instant recall of these kinds of facts gives learners the edge for solving problems quickly and efficiently. Difficulties arise when the facts are not properly understood. Knowing that 6 and 4 make 10, or that 4 times 7 equals 28, is useful only if children understand the meanings behind these facts. Similarly, children often learn a single method for finding the solution to a range of problems. But what happens when that one method is forgotten? Facts and methods are essential building blocks towards mathematical success, but are only useful if they support children's independent approaches to problem-solving.

Developing cumulative understanding

Mathematics is a hierarchical area of learning. We would not ask children to think in double-digit numbers before they are confident with numbers to 20. Similarly, we would not teach equivalent fractions if a child did not understand simple fractions. Many children leave Key Stage 1 without having grasped the concepts and there is often little time in Key Stage 2 to address cumulative gaps from earlier levels of learning.

Making numerical connections

How do you see the problem of 5 times 4? Do you see it as 4 + 4 + 4 + 4 + 4? Is your attention consciously drawn to the connection between multiplication and addition? Addition is the inverse (opposite) of subtraction. Multiplication is the inverse of division. Recognising connections between percentages, fractions and decimals enables us to problem-solve efficiently. Making numerical connections is crucial to long-term mathematical success. The logical thinkers amongst us will be better at it. But all learners can be shown how to connect concepts from the earliest stages. Were you actively helped to make connections, or did you go through schooling trying to understand isolated concepts? Help children to link mathematical ideas!

Estimating and self-checking

Connecting ideas relies on logic. From the earliest stages, children need to check mentally if they have sensible answers. This is particularly important now that modern mathematics relies on mental strategies.

A simple example – children need to realise that the answer to an addition or a multiplication problem will be greater than either of the numbers they started with. Recently, I asked some children if, when we add two numbers together, the answer would be more or less. Looks of astonishment suggested that they were unused to questions that required them to *think* without having to find the answer. Many children give an answer that is less when it should be more, and vice versa, because they are not applying logic to their thinking. Similarly many children mistakenly say that a quarter is bigger than a half, because four is greater than two. Those who have understood the concept of fractions reason that half must be bigger because the whole is shared into fewer parts.

Good mathematicians always estimate and know in advance their approximate answer and self-check to see if their actual answer is close to it.

Having a comprehensive approach to early number skills

Learning about numbers relies on a thorough understanding of each number and its relationship with others – the number before it, after it and so on. When teaching children at the earliest stages to understand numbers to 10, I encourage adults to take a thorough and comprehensive approach. For early number concepts to emerge securely, children should be able to do each of the tasks listed below.

Children need to:

- recognise each number from 0 to 10 independently
- write each numeral from 0 to 10
- make a set of objects to show values of 0 to 10
- place 0 to 9 number cards in order of value
- identify the 'missing' number when one is removed from the set
- say which number is '1 more' or '1 less' than a given number within the set
- say if any number up to 10 is smaller or larger than another (*Is 7 smaller or larger than 4?*)
- identify numbers in a given set – for example, the numbers more than 5.

Such activities invite learners to consider each number in relation to other numbers within its range (in this case, from 1 to 10, plus zero), all of which helps to secure understanding.

Children need also to apply numeracy knowledge to other aspects of mathematics, for example, money or shape. Activities for learning about numbers to 10 need to include shopping up to 10p and bar graphs with axes up to 10.

Instilling confidence and motivation

All children need success. Confidence is about 'having a go', and not feeling upset or embarrassed about getting it wrong. We should *expect* some incorrect answers, as part of the trial and error of learning. Children who understand that mistakes are often made, and that adults use misunderstandings to develop learning, continue to try. Confidence and motivation depend on how adults respond to children's attempts.

Try the following strategies:

- always say something positive about a response before pointing out that the answer is not what you are looking for
- praise the fact that the child has responded with something
- use the response to analyse confusions. Errors inform teaching and learning
- decide if there is a need to address areas of confusion as a whole class, group or individual approach.

Some children may get an answer almost right and appear to have applied the right strategy. They just need to think again. Others may be nowhere near, indicating that they have not grasped the basic principles of the problem. Children may lose heart altogether if what they are doing seems to be continually wrong, lacking interest or both.

Consider the following ideas for retaining children's motivation:

- presenting work that is lively and promotes interest
- using the names of children in the group as numeracy examples wherever possible (for example, John has 5 sweets, and gives 1 to Emma)
- ensuring that all learners are included
- praising pupil's responses and clearly valuing individual effort
- promoting success for each learner according to their personal terms of reference, even if this does not match the success of others
- laughing with pupils and having fun
- making mathematics relevant to children's current lives
- having a sense of purpose and ensuring that children know the objectives of every lesson and why they are learning and doing that particular task
- having a clear theme and sticking to it so that children are not confused.

Of course, children cannot be brimming with confidence and bursting with motivation 100 per cent of the time. Hopefully some of the ideas will help to keep pupils switched on.

Including all pupils

How do we include the full range of learners all or most of the time? Inclusion presents challenges. Consider the National Curriculum statements for inclusion:

> Schools have a responsibility to provide a broad and balanced curriculum for all pupils. The National Curriculum is the starting point for planning a school curriculum that meets the specific needs of individuals and groups of pupils. [There are] three principles that are essential to developing a more inclusive curriculum:
>
> A. Setting suitable learning challenges
>
> B. Responding to pupils' diverse learning needs
>
> C. Overcoming potential barriers to learning and assessment for individuals and groups of pupils. (DFEE/QCA 1999: 67)

Access is the open door to learning. Access ensures that all barriers that could limit or prevent any child benefiting from the curriculum have been removed. Language is one example. If in a numeracy lesson the explanation of a concept is beyond a child's understanding, then access disappears. Children who access the curriculum feel that they belong. Those who don't may well feel that the door is closed to them, and that they are not part of the learning experience.

Every child must have suitable challenges to respond to. If a child can only understand double-digit numbers, then the response to a question involving numbers over 1,000 is doomed. Challenges can also be too easy. When 'safe' questions are asked too often, learning will progress too slowly.

Some children need very tiny steps as their level of challenge. Others can take huge strides. What matters is that challenges are matched to what individual learners can cope with and still experience success, as well as retain confidence and motivation. It's about knowing the learners!

Diversity extends to every learning environment. In most classrooms there are children for whom English is an Additional Language. Most classrooms also have some children with different special educational needs. In some cases, children may have an Individual Education Plan. Able children may also have different needs. Diversity influences teaching in every classroom and, because some children learn differently, is about differences in learning style. Children learn in different ways:

- by rote
- by investigation
- pictorially or graphically (visually)
- in group discussion (speaking and listening)
- by using ICT.

Some children prefer to look at pictures and diagrams because they are visual learners. To some extent rote learning is necessary in all subjects, especially in numeracy, to enable efficient problem-solving. Recalling multiplication tables and number bonds to 10 speeds up mental calculation. Rote learning alongside understanding has its place.

Investigation involves a different approach to learning. Children may investigate prime numbers, multiples of numbers or square numbers. Investigation is a journey of mathematical discovery, during which learners find out for themselves and reach conclusions. They may discover, having investigated square numbers to 100, that the differences between each number follows the pattern of odd numbers (5, 7, 9, 11). They should make connections and ponder the question '*Why?*'

Others learn better through talk because they are social learners. Others prefer to learn through ICT. Yet others prefer word-based explanations. The thinkers may take a long time to respond because that is their learning style – to think.

Whatever the range of needs, a broad spectrum of tasks and activities in mathematics should address the individual learning styles of all children.

Problem-solving and thinking

Mathematics is about thinking. School mathematics is so geared towards getting through all of the units in the National Numeracy Strategy that time for children to develop their thoughts and to make connections is limited. For too many pupils, isolated bits of numerical knowledge do not develop effectively as part of *learning*. Processing a problem into a multiple of sums also involves thought. Does this problem involve addition, subtraction, multiplication or division and in what order? Children need time to connect ideas and to consider the most efficient problem-solving operations.

Making mathematics relevant to life

Chapter 1 made the point that mathematics is for life, and is not simply a school subject. Children cannot prepare themselves for a lifetime of mathematics if they do not practise for it through life-simulated and problem-solving opportunities.

Ensuring mathematical language is understood

Mathematics has its own terminology that can prevent access for many learners if not thoroughly explained. Consider the following: vertices, perpendicular, fraction, decimal, pentagon, translation. Such terms are specific to mathematics and essential to its understanding. Success depends on fusing both the language and the concepts as mathematical learning develops. Language is a major feature throughout this book.

Using mathematics to develop social and communication skills

Mention has been made of the need to address diversity in learning styles, with talk as one example. Mathematics lessons should involve as much pupil talk as possible.

Talking about problems can help children to:

- examine why different answers to a problem may be wrong
- explore different ways of approaching the same problem – assist some children to develop their range of methods
- develop the language of mathematics
- extend connections between concepts.

With regard to social skills and communication, mathematically focused talk helps children to:

- explain their views to others
- reflect on and consider the views of others
- use what others have said to challenge their own thinking.

Developing active learners

Consider the attributes of active and passive learners as shown in Figure 2.1.

The ACTIVE learner	The PASSIVE learner
Questions, challenges and evaluates	Accepts information without question
Is involved in decision-making	Is content for others to make decisions
Links new with known knowledge/ideas	Often has isolated areas of knowledge
Thinks and makes conceptual connections	Rarely makes connections
Places self at centre of learning process	Is on periphery of learning process

Figure 2.1 Attributes of active and passive learners

Children need to pull, push, stretch and twist pieces of information and link it to other information until it emerges as real, long-term learning. Active learners do this by questioning, challenging, manipulating and evaluating information. Active learners are also problem-solvers.

What happens in mathematics lessons?

The National Primary Strategy now includes the original numeracy and literacy strategies, that have been updated to the renewed Primary Framework (DfES 2006). For clarity I will refer to the National Numeracy Strategy (NNS).

What are primary schools aiming for?

Core areas of learning in the NNS Framework for Teaching (DfEE 1999a) and the renewed Framework (DfES 2006) are summarised below. They illustrate average expectations at age 11 (end of Year 6).

Children should:

- have a sense of the number system, to approximate that 547 is just over a half of 1,000, and 9,874 is just under 10 per cent of 100,000

- know key facts – for example, number bonds, multiplication tables and halving and doubling

- use known facts to figure out answers mentally

- calculate efficiently, mentally or on paper, drawing from a range of calculation strategies

- make sense of number problems and recognise the operations needed to solve them

- explain methods and reasoning, using the correct mathematical terms

- judge that their answers are reasonable and have strategies for checking

- suggest suitable units for measuring and make sensible estimates of measurements

- explain and make predictions from information presented on graphs, charts, diagrams and tables.

Note the verbs used – to 'have a sense of', 'recognise', 'explain', 'judge' – all these rely on understanding. The expectations are high, even for pupils of average ability and above. For those in the lower average range and especially those with special educational needs, the objectives will be achieved to a greater extent where teaching has regard to the principles explored in the previous chapter.

How is the daily mathematics lesson structured?

A key feature of the NNS is a daily mathematics lesson of between 45 and 60 minutes, depending on children's ages. Each lesson should involve:

- whole-class teaching for some of the time
- some group, pair and individual work as appropriate
- an emphasis on oral and mental strategies
- lively and interactive approaches to problem-solving.

The structure of each lesson generally involves the following:

- for 5–10 minutes, a mental warm-up with whole class
  - develop oral skills
  - practise instant recall of number facts
- for 30–40 minutes, the main teaching activity, as a whole class, in groups or pairs or individually
  - introduce new topic
  - consolidate/extend previous work
  - do group work, often organised by ability
- for 10–15 minutes, a plenary with the whole class
  - do an informal assessment of what has been learned (this is a chance to sort out confusion)
  - summarise key ideas
  - make connections with other work
  - set homework.

The TA role in the daily mathematics lesson

You might have agreed strategies to help pupils participate during planning discussions with class teachers.

During the mental warm-up you might:

- prompt children who need it
- support and encourage responses from shy or reticent children
- support children with learning difficulties
- support children with other forms of special educational need – a visual or hearing impairment, or physical disability
- help children to use specific resources and tools for independence, for example, an ICT programme, or a number line.

During the main part of the lesson you might:

- work with identified groups
- explain tasks
- keep children focused

- help to maintain pace
- remind children of main teaching points
- help children to respond correctly to the teacher's instructions
- question children and encourage their participation
- promote understanding of mathematical vocabulary
- observe and note common difficulties or mistakes to be addressed later.

During the plenary you might:

- monitor the responses of particular children
- prompt children to explain their strategies and methods
- prepare children and enable them to give feedback on the work they have been doing in the main part of the lesson.

You may be wondering how to fit it all in. You can't attend to everything at the same time. The TA role is most efficient when there have been prior discussions with class teachers on how to respond to the range of needs. You may feel, having looked at the above list, that there will be tensions between some aspects of your role, for example, between ensuring understanding and maintaining pace or between helping children to respond and encouraging independence. It's a question of balance. Pace is important, but not at the cost of understanding. Some children might need catch-up time outside mathematics lessons. And, while we must help children respond to instructions and tasks, their responses must be as independent as possible if real learning is to happen.

Encouraging independent learning

Working alongside teachers, your role is to help as many children as possible engage with learning. Independence is key, not least because effective learning depends on making decisions and taking responsibility. An independent learner is an active learner (as shown in Chapter 2). Independent learning is as much child led as adult led, more so as children mature. We all know children who rarely complete tasks unless prompted throughout each stage by an adult. Independence must be fostered from the start and developed throughout the Key Stages. Supporting adults need to make sensitive decisions on how best to help children be independent learners.
   A few pointers:

- never do for children what they can do themselves
- encourage children to use mathematical tools, such as number lines and tables squares, to recognise when they are needed and to get them out independently and model how to use such tools
- never sit beside an individual child longer than necessary
- avoid completing work for children.

It is difficult to maintain the brisk pace required by the NNS while promoting independence. But if we do not promote it, there is a danger that achievement (perhaps prompted by an adult) will be short term rather than long term and real.

Promoting key skills through mathematics

Pupils are expected to study the following topic areas in mathematics:

- at Key Stage 1 – number, shape, space and measures, handling data
- at Key Stage 2 – number, shape, space and measures, handling data
- at Key Stages 3 and 4 – number and algebra, shape, space and measures, handling data.

There is also a requirement to teach 'using and applying mathematics' in each topic area. Although algebra itself is not taught formally until Key Stages 3 and 4, the thinking skills that pupils use for algebra need to be taught in and through Key Stage 1 number work.

Mathematics can also be used to help promote spiritual, moral, social and cultural development:

- spiritual – helping pupils obtain insight into the infinite through mathematical principles, natural forms and patterns
- moral – using logical reasoning to consider consequences of decisions
- social – pupils working together productively on tasks and activities
- cultural – how thought contributes to our culture and is central to our technological future

and key skills:

- communication – learning to express ideas and methods precisely
- appreciation of number – applying knowledge, skills and understanding
- ICT – using graphic packages and spreadsheets to present and analyse data
- working with others – in group discussions and activities
- improving own learning and performance – through logical thinking, concentration and analytical approaches to problem-solving

Mathematics implicitly includes and develops thinking skills, financial capability, enterprise and entrepreneurial skills and work-related learning. The key skills are expected to develop alongside mathematical skills.

Moving from mental to written methods and using calculators

Not everyone will approach a problem in the same way, but some methods are more efficient than others. We need to approach a problem mentally before we consider using written methods or the calculator. Even then, a final mental check to see if an answer is sensible or not is always necessary.

Consider the three strategies.

1 *Mental methods* – In order to add 81 and 29 you might add 80 and 20, then 1 and 9, and then add 100 and 10 to make 110. Or, you may decide to add 81 and 30 (because 29 is 1 less than 30), and then subtract 1 from the total, to give 110. Such operations should be easily achievable for most people by using mental methods.

2   *Written methods and jottings* – Written notes are often necessary when the memory can't hold each part of the computation process. How would you add 487 and 356? It may be that you can hold each stage of the computation process in your memory. Some people would need to jot down their workings out. They may add 400 and 300 to make 700, then 80 and 50 to make 130, then 7 and 6 to make 13, jotting each sub-total, before adding all three together to total 843. But jottings and written methods should only be used when the complexity of the computation extends beyond an individual's mental capabilities. People with poor memories need to jot down as they go. Others can hold many sub-totals in their head. Written methods must never be taught without the mental strategies being thoroughly understood.

3   *Use of calculators* – The calculator is an efficient tool but can never replace the brain. There are times when a complex computation merits a calculator but calculators are not included in the NNS objectives for Key Stage 1, as mental strategies are still being developed. Calculators play a key role in subjects such as history, geography and science. They allow children to make effective use of data and compute quickly using numbers with several digits. There is no point in struggling to work out 26 per cent of the total of 252, 2,394 and 14,536 when a calculator can do the job in a fraction of the time. Having used the calculator our sense of the number system should kick in to check if the answer seems sensible.

Children should be able to:

- think mentally first
- decide if they need rough jottings as memory holders
- use formal written methods if complex
- use a calculator for very large or complex computations
- check mentally if the answer they have arrived at seems reasonable.

The Foundation Stage

Nursery level

In the nursery children are playing at mathematics, but focused play is preparation for the serious business of learning. At this stage children have opportunities to get excited about mathematics.

In the nursery the principles outlined in Chapter 2 can be embedded, and children's positive attitudes and early concepts can be established. At this stage all children can experience success and the key skills should kick off to a positive start.

What should be achieved during the Foundation Stage?

Curriculum guidance for the Foundation Stage, referred to as the Early Learning Goals (DfEE/QCA 2000) outlines what should be taught. These now relate directly to the renewed Primary Framework (DfES 2006). A Foundation Stage profile is completed for every child at the end of Reception, summarising the starting points for:

- numbers as labels for counting
- calculating
- shape, space and measures.

Strategies that can support achievement of the Early Learning Goals are discussed in the sections below.

Say and count the number names in order in familiar contexts

Children are introduced to stories and number rhymes that offer opportunities to say numbers in sequence. They should recite numbers in order, forwards and backwards, first 1 to 5, then up to 10, to 15 and to 20, as and when they are ready. This is a rare situation when we ask children to learn by rote without complete understanding. The objective is to learn the sequence of numbers, and to know their names. Secure understanding of each number follows later.

Count reliably up to 10 everyday objects

Use a range of objects for children to apply counting skills – counters, sweets, fruit. Try not to confuse the attribute that they are acquiring (number), by having others that get in the way. Also:

- try not to place objects always in rows – vary their positions
- start with 5 objects, and only move to 10, when secure
- make sure that children give one number name to each object being counted – model how to move the finger over each number.

Children need to understand what a number means. What is counting? The word 'count' is a verb so clapping and jumping help the counting process, as do fingers. What is meant by '5'? Relate numbers to values so that pupils realise that number 5 is of greater or lesser value than other numbers.

Introduce estimation – ask children how many they think is in a set without counting, then check. After a while children should recognise small sets of objects (below 5) without counting. They should also understand the idea of '0'.

Once children have got used to counting 1s, count in 2s and 3s. Some children may need to 'jump over' objects visually, to see that they are not counting every number in the sequence. Use alternate colours to support the counting sequence, for example red, then blue, to count in twos.

Recognise numerals 1 to 9

Numerals are the written form of numbers 1 to 9. Number 7 has one numeral. Number 634 has three. Children need to recognise the shapes and relate each to its name.

They could be helped to do this by:

- seeing numerals around school on displays, walls, etc. in different sizes
- sorting number cards
- playing games such as Snap, Pairs and Bingo, as illustrated in Figure 4.1
- matching number cards to sets of objects and pictures
- playing 'Hunt the numeral' to find, from numeral cards hidden round the classroom, the one that matches a set of objects
- picking out given numeral cards from a selection placed on the carpet.

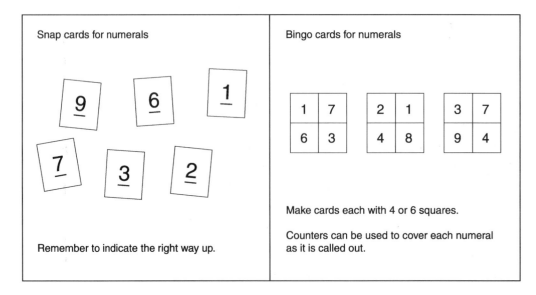

Figure 4.1   Games for recognising numerals

Like letters, numerals differ in only the slightest details, or in orientation, for example 6 and 9. Reversals when trying to write numerals are common at this stage. Think how each numeral differs and help children to focus on the differences.

Use language such as 'more/less', 'greater/smaller', 'heavier/lighter' to compare two numbers or quantities

This objective is preparation for measurement. There are no standard units – children use hands and feet, buckets, bowls and jugs, sticks and lengths of string.
During the Foundation Stage children need to develop:

- the concepts to do with measurement
- the language used to describe measurement.

Measurement includes time, weight and mass, capacity and length. Activities may include:

- Capacity – filling and emptying bowls, jugs and other different sized containers with liquid, and talking as they do it. The role of the adult is to ask the right questions that prompt thoughtful responses. *Which jug holds more/most? Why do you think that? Is that bowl full or empty? How many more cupfuls do you think will make it full?*

- Time – sequencing is a major concept of time. Children need to talk about the day's activities, days of the week, seasons and birthdays, and simple clock time (analogue only). Time language might include: 'next', 'after', 'before', 'first' and so on. Talking about events in the past or future provides opportunities to develop verb tenses, as these are implicit within the concept of time.

- Weight – children should be weighing a range of objects: plastic letters, toys, counters, pencils, rubbers and so on. Language is crucial: *Which is heavier/heaviest? How many counters weigh the same as the toy car?*

- Length – children use hands and feet to measure themselves and other objects. They could also use each other's hands and feet. Objects that are not straight can be measured by length of string.

Remember that, at this initial stage, the adult's role is to develop the concepts and the language through which they are labelled and described. Children are being introduced to the ideas of measurement ready for later work using standard units.

Through practical discussion, begin to use the vocabulary involved in adding and subtracting, finding one more or one less than a number from 1 to 10, and relate addition to combining two groups of objects, and subtraction to taking away.

I've placed the three 'number' objectives together here so that the links between them can be more easily appreciated. The important phrase is 'through practical discussion'. Once children can count beyond 10 the objective is to start to understand what numbers actually mean. The idea is to prepare children for formal addition and subtraction methods, and the mental approaches to computation in Key Stage 1. Activities should involve number-based talk, using interactive apparatus and objects.

The importance of language cannot be overstressed. It may come as a surprise to note the range of words and phrases to do with adding and subtracting in Reception. Using the words 'add', 'more', 'sum', 'total', 'altogether', we might ask:

- *How many do we have when we add 1 and 3?*

- *What is the sum of 2 and 4?*

- *Add one more. How many does that make altogether?*

Using the words 'one less', 'difference between', 'take away' and 'fewer than', we might ask:

- *What is one less than 4?*

- *What is the difference between 3 and 5?*

- *When we take 3 away from 5 how many are left?*

- *What is 2 fewer than 7?*

Finding 'one less than' or 'one more than' a given number is difficult for many learners. Focus on the language and make activities multi-sensory.
   You might:

- Place 10 objects in a row. Then count along to 5. Point to the next object, and count on to 6. Say together 'One more than 5 is 6.' Focus on the vocabulary that describes the activity as you model it, 'next', 'count on' and so on. Do similar activities with number cards.

- Show children how to 'jump' from one number to the next to represent 'one more'. Encourage children to state the outcome of each jump – for example, '7 is one more than 6.' Reverse the activity by jumping backwards. Draw each 'jump' in colour.

- Practise the same objective orally. Ask the child to pick from a selection of number cards 'one more than 3', or 'one less than 5'.

- As children become confident, check that they can apply the same concept at different levels: 'one more than' progresses to 'two or three more than'.

Consider how we learn to combine groups of objects and add others to a set. Draw addition problems as shown in Figure 4.2 so that pupils can 'see' them.

Introduce the full range of groupings for numbers to 10 (9 and 1, 2 and 8, 3 and 7 and so on) and show children that each pair adds up to the same (2 + 8 is the same as 8 + 2). This is the start of what we often call 'number bonds'. While at the Reception stage we do not expect children to know each pair of groupings, the idea that different pairs can total 10 needs to be grasped.

Activities for combining groups could include:

- drawing the range of groups using different pictures and objects
- counting and moving objects between the two groups to show that if one set becomes bigger, the other must become smaller.

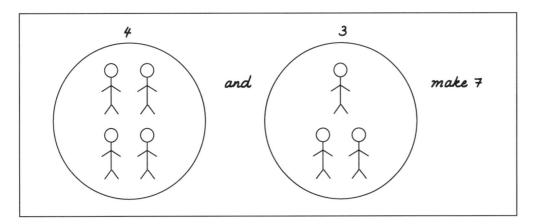

Figure 4.2   Combining groups of objects

This is the start of algebraic thinking, and the later skill of balancing number values at each side of an equation, for example $X + 6 = 10$ or $10 - X = 6$. At the Foundation Stage children need to recognise that adding and taking away are related and use simple language to describe the relationships, for example:

- *6 from 10 leaves 4* is related to *4 from 10 leaves 6*
- *6 and 4 make 10* is related to *4 and 6 make 10*.

As a start to relating subtraction to 'taking away', you might get children to:

- draw sets of objects, and cross out what is taken away
- with a set of objects, give some away, eat some, lose some. Demonstrate different ways of making the set less than you started with.

Make activities visual so that the numerical concepts and the language are linked.

A principle outlined in Chapter 2 features strongly at the Foundation Stage, comprehensive understanding of early number. Without it, children can never be secure with larger numbers.

With regard to number, let's summarise what children should be well on their way to doing by the end of the Reception year. The majority should be:

- recognising each numeral from 1 to 9, and zero as 'o'
- writing each numeral correctly from memory
- compiling sets of any amount, using different objects, up to 10
- finding the 'missing' number card when one is taken away
- sequencing number cards in order of value, smallest to largest or vice versa
- finding one more or one less than any number up to 10
- adding two groups of objects together

- taking a given amount away from a number group (e.g. 6 from 9), and counting how many are left

- matching pairs of numbers with the same value, 3 and 7 with 2 and 8

- solving simple problems with number values up to 10.

Children who can do most of the above will have a good kick-start for Key Stage 1. Yet even with the best teaching and support, we know that not all will achieve the above skills, and some will need additional time to develop them throughout Year 1. It is crucial that they do, and that all adults have high expectations for every child.

Talk about, recognise and create simple patterns

Look for patterns in the home, school, street and shops. People who are good at mathematics are good at seeing patterns of shapes and numbers. See Figure 4.3 for some examples.

Pattern	Pupils might recognise
dog cat fish dog cat fish dog	the words 'dog cat fish' repeat
a b c d e	the alphabet
1 3 5 7 9	odd numbers
4 8 16 32	multiples of 4
120 100 80 60 40	subtraction by 20

Figure 4.3 Patterns in numbers and letters

Dealing with patterns in mathematics is a bit like appreciating rhythm in music. Some people are instantly cued in. Others need to be trained to 'see' missing parts of a sequence, or parts in a particular order.

When working with pattern:

- talk about the connecting sequence. *Is it every other shape or number? Is the sequence increasing in size or value, or decreasing?*

- present number sequences that are within the level of learning that children can manage (up to 10)

- draw lots of patterns, and get children to be creative

- arrange coloured counters and different objects into sequential patterns

- children could work in pairs to create patterns for their partner to continue

- children could draw pictures of the patterns around them, for example on wallpaper – obtain rolls to look at

- children could use different mediums to create their patterns – drawing, painting, tactile objects, making a collage.

Working with patterns can be fun as children enjoy colour and different mediums.

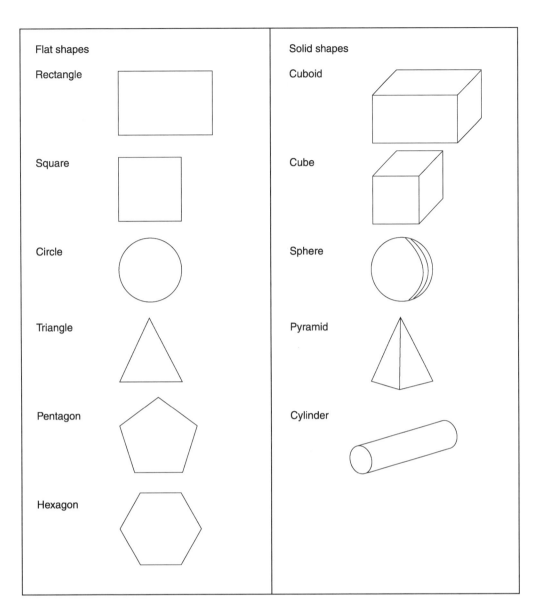

Figure 4.4 Flat and solid shapes

Use language, such as 'circle' or 'bigger', to talk about and describe the shape and size of flat and solid shapes

Talk about the attributes of each shape. Relate each flat shape to its solid cousin. *Why are they related? What is similar about the circle, the sphere and the cylinder? How is the cube different from the cuboid?* Ask questions by examining different examples of each shape. *Are all sides of the rectangle the same? How many long ones/short ones are there? Are all sides of the square the same or different?* We might also ask children which are the most common shapes around us, and why. Shapes are fun to explore using the environment and will encourage children to be observant when they are out and about shopping, on holiday or at the dentist.

Simply knowing the words for things does not mean that children have developed a concept of it. So many other attributes, for example colour, can get in the way of understanding. Collect different examples of the same basic shape, and talk about the attributes that characterise it. A triangle is a triangle because it has three straight sides and three corners (we're not into *angles* at this stage), and if a shape does not have these attributes, it is not a triangle. All shapes that fall into the same category do not have to be identical.

Activities to develop understanding of shape might include:

- asking startling questions to encourage thought. *Why is a door not a circle? Why are cereal packets usually cuboids?*

- getting pairs of children to ask each other questions. Children need to develop their questioning skills for all areas of learning

- sorting pictures of shapes into categories and talking about why all of the sets are rectangles, squares, triangles and so on

- experimenting to see which shapes fit together with no spaces between. *Why?*

- playing games such as Snap, Pairs, Bingo and Dominoes using cards with the basic shapes on them

- making shapes and talking about which ones are the easiest or hardest to make. *Why?*

- collecting different shapes and trying to find some unusual ones

- talking about common shapes that can be seen in the world around us, for example, rectangles, squares or triangles in schoolrooms, homes, churches or shops.

Using everyday words to describe position

Where are you now? What language would you use to describe where you are? Common words that describe position and direction include prepositions: 'up', 'down', 'behind', 'in the middle', and so on. Children need to describe their own position in relation to their surroundings, and those of other children and objects.

Activities could include:

- Working with arrows to describe simple position words such as 'up', 'down', 'left', 'right', 'diagonal'

- Talk that instructs children to: 'turn to the right/left', 'go to the beginning/end of the row', 'go to the opposite corner of the room' (could be Simon Says)

- Drawing lines that are horizontal, vertical or diagonal (using simple language)

- Following and giving instructions on direction and movement in PE.

The main aim is for children to describe themselves and objects around them in terms of position and movement ready for later work on angles and coordinates.

Use developing mathematical ideas to solve practical problems

Problems make mathematics live. One child I worked with was trying to make sets of 2 (as a start to simple multiplication and to count in 2s). He insisted on counting each set as elephants going to a zoo. He placed each set of 2 in a bag to be 'flown' to each of 5 'zoos'. Representation helped him to work out how many zoos were needed to house the elephants (and that 5 sets of 2 make 10).

At the Foundation Stage, children have opportunities for roleplay, but this may be reduced or ceased altogether in Year 1. Make the most of opportunities in Reception for problem-solving through shopping in different contexts. Pupils need to become familiar with basic coins.

Stretch children's thinking with puzzles. 'How many rectangles?' can help children see different-sized shapes that appear hidden within and among other rectangles. 'Which ones match?' can help children see similarities despite a difference in size.

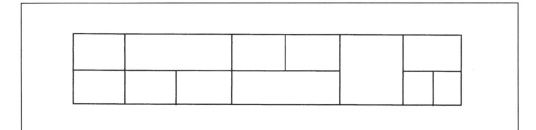

Figure 4.5   How many rectangles?

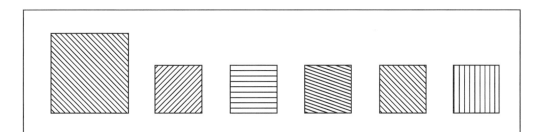

Figure 4.6   Which ones match?

Children also need to experience different types of mathematical problems:

- word problems – 6 ducks are swimming in the pond. 3 more ducks join them. How many ducks are in the pond altogether?

- finding possibilities – How many ways can you exit the maze in Figure 4.7?

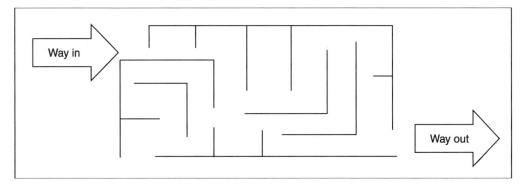

Figure 4.7   How many ways out of the maze?

- logic puzzles – using clues to solve problems (I am a shape with 3 sides. I am a number less than 8 but more than 6).

- finding rules and patterns types of problems – for example working out the pattern for adding steps in a building as shown in Figure 4.8

- visual and diagrammatic types of problems – how many triangles, as shown in Figure 4.9.

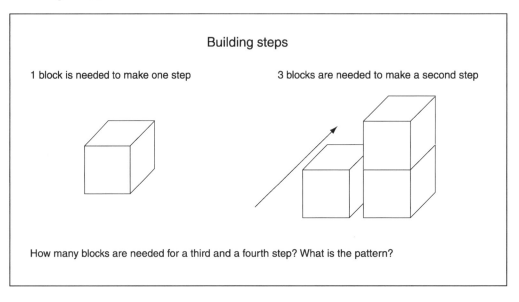

Figure 4.8 What's the pattern for adding steps?

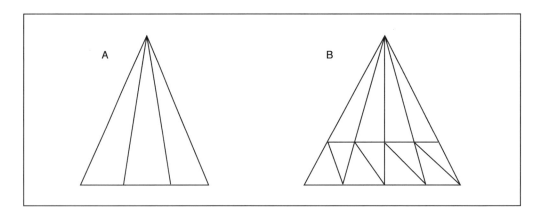

Figure 4.9 How many triangles can you see?

How we respond to each type of problem depends on how we think, but children need to experience each type. Most activities at the Foundation Stage are problem-solving as formal mathematics has not yet kicked in and most activities are contextualised. Encourage children to think strategically, rather than apply random guesswork.

Linking 'good practice' principles

It is important to link four of the principles already mentioned when helping children in the Foundation Stage:

- Language – We can't always plan precisely the words we use in speech and, if we tried to, our language would be anything but spontaneous. But vocabulary must be descriptive and link to an activity to help children understand the mathematical concepts involved. Talk labels action and gives it meaning. The mathematical vocabulary listed in the NNS is a useful reference.

- Comprehensive understanding of number is crucial in the Foundation Stage – A narrow perception of number will severely limit children's potential to learn from later mathematical experiences.

- Cross-curricular application of mathematics – At this stage there are no discrete subject areas, so it is easier to blend mathematics into any task.

- Key skills – Social and communication skills must be initiated early. Children who cannot take turns and communicate effectively will struggle later.

Activities to support parents

Parents often ask what they can do to help their child and TAs may be asked to give advice. The questions in the following suggestions may be helpful. Remember that the focus should always be on concepts and the language that describes them.

- In the kitchen – *Which pan is the smallest/biggest? How many spoonfuls of flour?*
- At bath time – *What will float/sink? Which is the smaller/bigger towel?*
- Getting dressed – *Which clothes do I put on first/next/last?*
- Having breakfast – *Which cereal bowl? Is it big enough? Is the milk bottle full, half-full or empty?*
- At the table – *What shape are the plates? How many cups/mugs do we have? How many pieces shall we cut the cake into?*
- Storytime – *Which book shall I read? How long is it? How many pages is it? Is it longer than the last book I read?*
- Our house – *What shapes are our windows, doors, clock, rug or garden?*

All aspects of mathematics can found in the home, and parents will enjoy reinforcing their children's skills once they know how. Simple games such as Snap and Bingo can also be played at home to reinforce concepts of number, shape or pattern. Most children have experiences of mathematics out of school: ages of people in the family, the number on the door, lottery numbers, telephone numbers and so on. We need to keep parents informed and try to involve them as much as possible.

During the Foundation Stage mathematical experiences can be folded into any aspect of the school day. Routines such as taking the register, changing for PE, fruit at playtime and lining up to go out offer opportunities to develop mathematical ideas and language.

CHAPTER 5

Key Stage 1

This chapter focuses on teaching and learning for children in Years 1 and 2, taking the objectives from the NNS as the starting point for suggestions and practical activities.

Year 1

The demands for Year 1 are heavy, yet time must be found to reinforce insecure learning from Reception. Children who have not grasped the language and concepts from the Foundation Stage will be disadvantaged unless they have opportunities to revisit what has been taught. From Year 1, children start to follow the National Curriculum, but they continue to experiment with number, shape, position, pattern and problem-solving.

The following sections explore the main objectives for Year 1.

Count reliably to at least 20 objects

Activities for counting to 10 objects could be recycled. The key word is *reliably*. Many children when counting higher quantities lose their place. They may be reciting the numbers accurately but the eye is not in tandem with the 'jumping finger'.

Count on and back in 1s from a small number, in 10s from and back to 0

Children need to say the number they are starting with, then count on from it (not always from number 1). The counting sequence must be secure before children practise from different starting points. A number line helps children to keep track. Children also need to count in 2s and 3s. Jumping along number lines helps them to adjust to the difference between counting in 1s and counting in different groupings. Colours help children to see patterns as they count. Counting in different groupings prepares children for work on multiplication and odd and even numbers. Once children start to count in groups they need to see patterns of missing numbers, for example, that counting in groups of 5 misses out 4 numbers each time.

Counting in 10s to 100 and back to 0 introduces the idea that 10 and 20 are part of a bigger number system. Using a 100-number square helps children to see that:

- each number ending in 0 is at the end of a line
- each set of 10 is the same length (and value)

- there are 10 numbers (units) in each set of 10
- there are 10 sets of 10 up to 100.

What else might you say about the patterns? Ask questions that make pupils think about patterns made by numbers. *Why is each set of 10 at the end of the line? Why are numbers ending in 5 in the same column?* Asking questions develops thinking.

Activities for counting in groups might include:

- colouring the 10s patterns on a 100-number square
- colouring the 5s, and other patterns
- colouring other columns (3s or 4s) and then asking what value they represent
- talking about the numbers and using apparatus to count each set of 10, to see that there are 10 sets of 10 in 100, 5 sets of 10 in 50 and so on.

Some children in Year 1 may start to understand two-digit numbers. Others will need to see different arrangements of 10s and units, as shown in Figure 5.1, to start to acquire the concept of place value. Place value features significantly as the start of a long process of understanding numbers, theoretically to infinity (billions?). If two-digit numbers are not understood, further place value can never be secure.

24 is 2 sets of 10 and 4 units.	36 is 3 sets of 10 and 6 units.
XXXXXXXXXX	XXXXXXXXXX
XXXXXXXXXX	XXXXXXXXXX
XXXX	XXXXXXXXXX
	XXXXXX

Figure 5.1 Arrangements of 10s and units to support understanding of place value

Read and write numerals from 0 to at least 20

Activities might include:

- selecting the correct cards when given numbers orally for example, *Find 18*
- matching numerals to pictures or objects with the same values, for example, matching 17 to a picture with 17 objects
- drawing sets of objects to match given amounts
- playing games, for example, Snap, Bingo and Dominoes
- partitioning 'teens' numbers into 10s and 1s, and recombining, to show how they become two-digit numbers (how 10 and 7 form 17).

Understand and use the vocabulary for comparing and ordering numbers

This objective is to do with place value. Children who have not grasped numbers to 20 need urgent intervention before they can work with two-digit numbers.

Activities for comparing and ordering two-digit numbers include:

- placing two-digit numbers in order, and asking children why 86 is of greater value than 61. Children should be able to state that there are more 10s in 86 than 61, and use reasoning to explain that 86 must be of greater value because 10s are worth more than units

- comparing numbers and saying which is more or less

- placing sets of numeral cards (from 0 to 9) together to form two-digit numbers (9 and 5 to form 95). Ask children which cards, when paired together, can form the highest value

- playing games, for example, place sets of number cards face down and ask children to pick one card in turn. Who can make a two-digit number with the most or least value?

- asking which number lies between 2 two-digit numbers, for example, 34 and 36

- talking about the range of vocabulary for comparing numbers: 'more', 'less', 'fewer', 'between', 'highest' or 'most value', 'lowest' or, 'least value'

- using the sign (=) for equality when comparing number values, play Snap games to signal matching values.

- practising ordinal numbers (1st, 2nd, 3rd). Use lining-up opportunities to develop ordinal sequence. Ordinal numbers can refer to time (first lesson, second lesson) as well as position (first place, second place in the queue).

Within the range 0 to 30 say the number that is 1 or 10 more or less than any given number

To say which number is '1 less' or '10 more' than any number, children must start to understand the number system. *Which number is 1 less than 27? Say the number that is 1 more than 16.* Children must now see that the 'one less' is taken from the units and the 'one more' is added to the units. They must know which digits in two-digit numbers represent units. *Which number is one more than 19? Which number is one less than 30?* These questions require understanding that numbers after those with 9 units subsume the last set of 10. Finding 1 more than 27 is easier than finding 1 more than 29. Include questions that make pupils think about the next set of 10.

Order numbers to at least 20 and position them onto a number track

This objective assesses understanding of number values. If pupils struggle, observe what they are doing. At which point is their ordering incorrect? Is it the number after 9? Do they need to secure combinations of 10?

Understanding addition and subtraction

From practically adding and taking away, children build from the general to the more specific as the start of 'proper' mathematics. Children need to understand the operations alongside the notation signs for addition and subtraction (+ and –), as well as the sign for equal (=). Understanding that $8 - 2 = 6$ is different from understanding, with objects in front of us, that if we take 2 away from 8 we are left with 6. Similarly, 9 + 6 = 15, thought through mentally, represents a considerable step forward from adding them together practically.

Simple numeracy is done mentally, although some children will need apparatus to enable them to 'see' what they are doing until they can deal with the abstraction. Children need to realise that:

- addition can be done in any order (4 + 13 is the same as 13 + 4)
- we can add more than two numbers (2 + 5 + 7 + 8)
- the answer to an addition will always be more than any of the individual numbers involved
- subtraction cannot be done in any order (14 – 5 does not equal 5 – 14)
- unlike addition, horizontal subtractions always work from left to right.

Ask questions that tease out key differences between each operation. No answers are needed. The aim is to promote logical thought. Such questions might include:

- *Is 21 + 16 the same as 16 + 21? Will the answer to this sum be larger or smaller than either of the two numbers?*
- *Is 26 – 13 the same as 13 – 26? Why not? What do you think will happen if we try to take a larger number from a smaller one?*

Later on children realise that we can subtract a larger number from a smaller one to obtain a minus number. (This is like the idea of a bank overdraft, but that concept is for Key Stage 2.) Year 1 pupils just need to understand that we can only take a smaller number from a larger one, but we can add a larger number to a smaller one.

Symbols stand for 'unknown' numbers. This is a start to understanding inverse operations. To find out which number to add to 13 to make 20, we need to subtract 13 from 20. The addition problem converts to a subtraction thought process. Vary the work so that the relationships between addition and subtraction can be fully grasped in Year 1. Play the 'Chain game'. This is an oral, small-group or pair activity that develops memory skills and understanding of addition and subtraction. Children have to remember the previous answer, as their number might form the next link in the 'chain'. This game can be played at different levels for less or more-able groups.

Child 1:   *I have 8. Who has 3 more?*
Child 2:   *I do – I have 11. Who has 6 less?*
Child 3:   *I do – I have 5. Who has 10 more?*
Child 4:   *I do – I have 15. Who has 2 more?*

This type of activity allows adults to observe which children have grasped the ideas and which haven't in order to plan reinforcement work.

Know by heart all pairs of numbers with a total of 10

This objective involves instant recall of addition and subtraction facts, often referred to as 'number bonds'. Rapid recall of number bonds to 10 (later to 20) enables efficient mental calculations with larger numbers. Children must understand the number bonds and be able to recall them. They could do oral activities:

- an adult says a number below 10 and a child states its 'partner' (Question: *What is the partner of 6 to make 10?* Answer: 4)
- children work in pairs to state partners to 10

or activities that use single-digit number or addition cards:

- Snap – two numbers that total 10 are turned together
- Dominoes – the last number put down has to be matched with a partner
- Match – match addition or subtraction cards with cards that have identical values, for example, 3 + 7 matches 7 + 3 or 14 − 4

or activities with dice:

- a dice with '+2' or '−1' could be used to vary the difficulty of the mental operations, for example, throwing 6, then 5, followed by −1 results in 10 and adds an extra dimension to the activity.

Children should be able to double and halve numbers to 10 and know that doubling is related to addition, while halving is related to subtraction. Language is the key – ensure that words such as 'subtract', 'add', 'half', 'double', 'less than' and 'more than' are fully understood. Ask thought-provoking questions such as 'If we double a number is it more or less than we started with?'

Strategies for mental calculations of addition and subtraction

Doing things the right way saves time and effort. We need to introduce children to the most efficient ways in which to perform mental operations.

Strategies for working efficiently include:

- placing the larger number before the smaller when adding two numbers together, for example, 14 + 3 is easier than 3 + 14
- using number facts related to 5 efficiently to partition and recombine, for example, 8 + 7 partitioned as 5 + 3 and 5 + 2 becomes 10 + 5 = 15
- using doubles facts to calculate 'almost doubles', for example, knowing that 5 + 5 = 10 allows us to work out 6 + 5 quickly by adding 1
- adding 9 to single-digit numbers by adding 10, then subtracting 1, thus, 7 + 9 = 7 + 10 = 17 − 1 = 16
- using patterns of calculations to stimulate thinking, for example, 'How would this subtraction pattern continue?' 10 − 1 = 9, 10 − 2 = 8.

Estimating

By the end of Year 1 many children have started to acquire that 'sense' of numbers and their values at a simple level and should estimate within a reasonable range. Start with up to five objects for children to estimate, then count. Then progress to 10, 15 and so on, including odd and even numbers to approximately 30. Make it a game for children to play in pairs, estimating each other's amounts.

Using measures to compare two lengths, masses or capacity by direct comparison, using uniform non-standard units

General vocabulary includes 'size', 'compare', 'guess', 'enough', 'too many' and 'too few'. More specific vocabulary about length, weight, mass and time might include words such as 'long', 'short', 'tall', 'heavier', 'lighter', 'full' and 'half full' and days of the week, months and seasons.

The emphasis in Year 1 is on uniformity, using non-standard units to start with. Children might use yogurt pots for measuring quantities, cubes for weights and straws for length. The units are uniform in the sense that they are of the same size or length. Children can now make statements such as '5 yogurt pots hold the same amount as 2 jugs,' or '3 straws are the same length as 1 ruler.'

Suggest suitable standard units to estimate and measure capacity, mass or length

Children should also start to estimate measurements using basic standard units, for example, state that 6 cups of water fill a 1 litre jug. Ask which objects children think are lighter or heavier, for example 30 cubes or 10 pencils, then weigh them to check their estimates. As far as time is concerned children should start to know the days of the week, months and seasons, linked to events in their own lives. Exploration of measurement using non-standard units helps to refine children's initial ideas ready for work on standard units. Children will soon begin to see measurement problems as more or less obvious.

Shape and space – describe features of 2-D and 3-D shapes

Talk about the attributes of each shape – corners, length and sides. Children need to construct shapes using everyday materials as models – cereal packets for cuboids, Toblerone or other chocolate boxes for talking about triangles and pyramids.

Work on symmetry begins as children fold paper shapes to form symmetrical patterns. Experiment with folding into halves and quarters, diagonally as well as up and down, exploring differences and similarities. Talk about the changes to develop understanding of symmetry. Think about the shapes shown in Figure 5.2. These have been folded symmetrically then opened out. *What shapes were the patterns originally? What did they become when folded, if different?*

Children also need to relate solid shapes to pictures using photographs and drawings. Work on shape and space also involves experimenting with things that turn, for example, wheels and windmills. Vocabulary includes words that describe position (over, under, above, below), direction (journey, left, right, up and down) and movement (full and half turns, slide, roll, stretch, bend, away from, towards). (Remember the NNS booklet on mathematical vocabulary.)

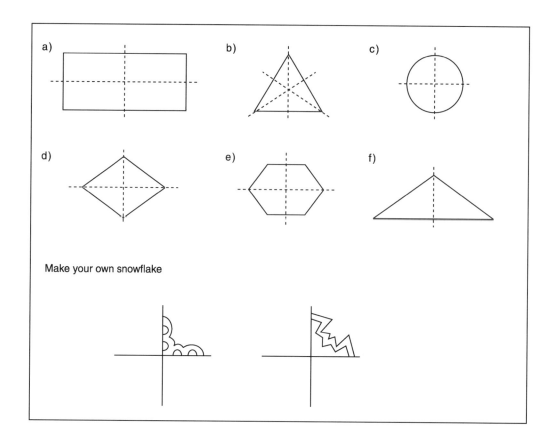

Make your own snowflake

Figure 5.2 Folding shapes to form symmetrical patterns

Children should now use their growing knowledge of numbers and their applications to design more creative patterns and sequences. *How would you continue these sequences?*

20 19 18 ____ ____ ____
0 5 ____ 15 ____ 25 30
2 4 6 ____ ____ ____ 14 ____ 18

Applying number work and solving problems

Implicit within the understanding of numbers are the applications that make mathematics relevant and meaningful. Application of number work involves solving puzzles and investigating statements. How might a Year 1 child respond to such questions as:

- *What can you tell me about the number 5?*

- *How can you change a square into a rectangle, and make your rectangle double the size of the square?*

- *Why can a sphere roll but a cube can't? Which other solid shape can roll?*

Children may give answers similar to the following

Facts about the number 5:
- *5 is half of 10*
- *2 and 3 make 5*
- *5 is 3 less than 8*

- *5 sweets cannot be shared equally*
- *we have a coin for 5p*
- *5 is 4 more than 1*
- *numbers ending in 5 are halfway along the 100 number square on every row.*

They may also reason that to make a square into a rectangle we need to make the two opposite sides longer, and the same length. To double the size of the square, they may conclude that the rectangle needs to be 'the same again' as the square, with the longer sides doubled. Similarly, pupils may reason that the sphere rolls because it has no edges and is round like a ball. The cube can't roll because its edges would stop it. Cubes can slide along smooth surfaces. Cylinders can roll but only one way because the ends are flat.

Children might come to these conclusions after they have investigated the problems. Asking the kinds of reasoning questions given above extends their thinking and invites them to use their growing knowledge creatively. You can also ask them to identify statements as true or false. And, if they say a statement is false, you can ask them to make it true. For example:

A triangle has 4 sides
Doors are often cuboids
15 is double 10

You could write the statements on cards and place them in a a a pile for children to pick up in turn. If they make the correct response they keep the card, and the child with the most cards wins.

Solving number problems

Children need to choose from a range of strategies. Success involves being able to use different methods for each mathematical operation. Encourage children to generate questions! For example, *How many ways can we make number 15? I have 17 sweets and eat 3. How many have I left?*

Using money

In Year 1 children still need opportunities for 'shopping', with talk on buying and selling, finding totals, giving change to at least 20p and recognising coins of different values. Previous practice of counting on in 1s, 2s, 5s and 10s should now be applied to money. Children could sort and match monetary values. For example they could:

- sort 5p, 2p, 1p, 20p, £1 and 50p into two groups: more than 10p and less than 10p

- match 5p + 5p, 5p + 2p and 10p + 10p to 7p, 20p or 10p.

Organising and using data

Lastly, children in Year 1 will be organising and interpreting simple data such as the dates of their birthdays, which they might put into a bar chart, as shown in Figure 5.3. They have to collect the data and construct axes for their bar chart. They also have to interpret other data and learn to 'read' this type of information.

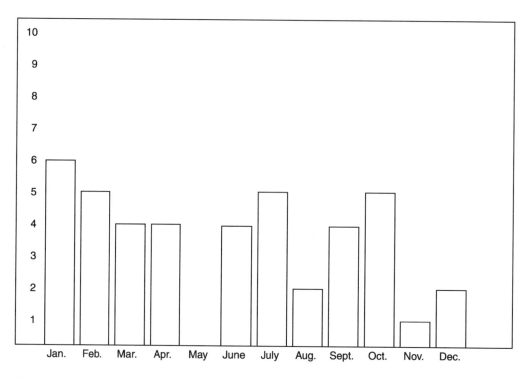

Figure 5.3   Bar chart of birthday months

Think about the knowledge a child needs to comprehend such information. Think about shape and space as well as number.

The easiest questions involve simply reading the chart, and might include:

- *How many class birthdays are in January (or March, or July)?*

More challenging questions might also involve addition, subtraction or both:

- *How many birthdays are in the months of January, February and March?*
- *How many more (or less) birthdays are in July than in September?*
- *How many more birthdays are in January, February and March, than in September, October and November?*

More challenging questions might be inferential (without clear-cut answers):

- *How many children may be able to have their parties out in the garden?*

By the end of Year 1 a huge store of language and mathematical knowledge has been built on to what children learned in the Foundation Stage. But many children will be way behind and will need 'catch-up' strategies (addressed later in the chapter).

Year 2

The following sections reflect the NNS teaching programme for Year 2 and offer practical strategies and activities for helping children to achieve the key objectives.

The main areas of learning for Year 2 are:

- the more precise use of mathematical language to describe and explain
- secure understanding of place value and numbers to 100
- more secure understanding of addition and subtraction as inverse operations
- introduction of multiplication and times tables
- use of appropriate operations to solve problems and the ability to explain how a problem was solved.

Mathematics by the end of Year 2 has moved on considerably but there should still be opportunities to reinforce Year 1 learning. What is covered in one year is expected to be secure by the following year. A flexible rolling programme allows children to explore areas of learning with the expectation that they will have consolidated them by the end of the following year through much revisiting.

Use of mathematical language

The language used in Reception and Year 1 to label and describe becomes much more specific in Year 2, further demonstrating the need for talk to ensure that children are linking new concepts to the relevant vocabulary. This point is amply illustrated in the booklet on mathematical vocabulary (DfEE 1999b) already referred to, and a 'must' for every adult involved with mathematics in schools.

Understanding numbers to 100

Year 2 children need to count to at least 100, forwards and backwards, and in 1s and 10s. They also need to be able to count up to 100 objects accurately, by grouping them systematically into 10s, 5s or 2s, as preparation for multiplication.

Children also need to recognise odd and even numbers to at least 30. They could do this by colouring in alternate numbers on a number square and talking about the effects. *What colour patterns are made? Which are the odd numbers? What do we notice about them? Why can we not share odd numbers of sweets between 2 friends?*

By counting on in 3s, 4s or 5s, pupils learn to appreciate patterns made by numbers, especially if activities are visual. Counting in different groupings prepares learners for multiplication and division work, especially if we ask thought-provoking questions such as:

- *When we count in 4s, how many sets of 4 are there when we reach 40, 80 or 100?*
- *Why are there twice as many sets of 4 in 80, as there are in 40?*

Extend activities around the 'true or false' theme, such as:

- *4 is an odd number*
- *the number 9 can be shared between 4 friends*
- *we can share 12 into 6 groups.*

Enhance the activity by asking children to make the false statements true.

Understanding place value to 100

One of the most difficult mathematical concepts is place value. Numbers to 20 are easily visual. Beyond 20 many children struggle. Children need to be able to read and write two-digit numbers and to partition them into 10s and units (29 into 20 and 9).

Activities for reading and writing two-digit numbers often include:

- reading aloud numbers using the 100-number square – in sequence as well as up and down the 10s or other columns
- using two-digit number cards – talk about what each number represents
- selecting given two-digit numbers from a set of number cards.

For partitioning two-digit numbers, activities might include:

- children pairing numerals (any number to 9) into given two-digit numbers – you say 59, they have to pair 5 with 9 in that order
- pairing 0 to 9 numeral cards to make two-digit numbers that are more or less – for example, any number less than 61 or any number more than 49
- changing the units to reduce or increase the value – from 65 to 61 or to 73
- changing the tens to reduce or increase the value – from 59 to 29 or to 89
- using apparatus to show the values of two-digit numbers, for example, arranging 3 10s and 4 units so that children can 'see' what 34 means.

Activities for ordering and comparing number values include:

- using the 100-number square to identify any number, for example, bigger than 45, or smaller than 83
- placing two-digit number cards in order of value
- rounding two-digit numbers up or down to the nearest 10 or 5
- finding the 'missing' two-digit number when one (or more) is taken away from a sequence, as illustrated below. Numbers need not be consecutive, nor need they start from 1.

  ___ 24 25 26 27 ___ 29 30 31 ___ ___ 34

  ___ 10 15 ___ 25 30 ___ ___ 45

Addition and subtraction as inverse operations

Provide practice with 'missing' double-digit numbers at different levels of challenge.
Simple examples:

$78 - ? = 58$
$? + 60 = 100$
$32 = 28 + ?$

Challenging examples:

$35 + ? = 45 + 10$
$35 + 25 = ? - 20$

Present the problems in different ways to encourage flexible thought, and to reinforce the inverse characteristics of addition and subtraction.

Multiplication as repeated addition

Consider the problem posed in Figure 5.4 and think about what it means.

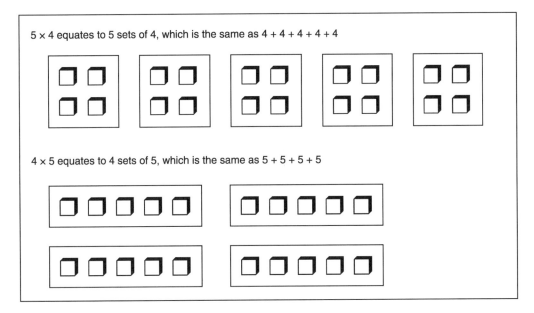

Figure 5.4   Multiplication as repeated addition

To understand multiplication children need to see the sets of 4 and 5 so that they can count them and see that they total 20, and that 5 sets of 4 mean the same as 4 sets of 5 because they add up to the same total. Year 2 also introduces the idea of division as sharing and the inverse of multiplication. These links are not obvious until 'seen'. Consider:

$$5 \times 14 = 70$$
$$70 \div 5 = 14$$
$$14 \times 5 = 70$$
$$70 = 5 \times 14$$

The same problem can be presented in different ways. Mathematical notation needs to be thoroughly grasped and children must acquire the range of vocabulary used to describe it. Activities might include:

- Matching inverse mathematical statements, for example, $4 \times 3 = 12$ matches with $12 \div 3 = 4$.
- Finding the odd one out from a set of linked mathematical statements.
- Transferring sums to problems or vice versa, and drawing them. For example, there are 8 squares of chocolate in 1 chocolate bar. How many are there in 6 bars? Children could draw the problem by sketching 1 bar and then 6, to compare the number of squares. They could work in pairs or groups for support.

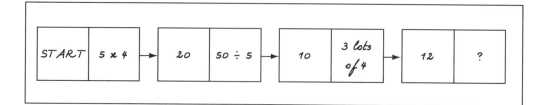

Figure 5.5 Dominoes with multiplication and division

- Drawing problems for different mathematical statements, for example, illustrating the problem 54 + 27 by setting out the tens and units in an array. This would support visual learners.

- Playing some of the games already discussed, such as Dominoes, Snap or Bingo. For Bingo, the 'caller' could call out the answers for children to identify the different statements that link to it, or vice versa (when you're designing Domino games, don't put the same answer on more than one card; that way the chain will not be broken until the last card is put down). See Figure 5.5. The games can focus on a particular set of tables or be random.

- Doing the same activities with doubling and halving to show that these are inverse operations.

Choosing and using appropriate operations to solve problems

By the end of Year 2 most children understand the links between:

- Addition and subtraction – inverse

- Multiplication and division – inverse

- Addition and multiplication – as 'more' concepts

- Subtraction and division – as 'less' concepts.

Without such understanding children will not be able to solve problems. Pupils also need to see multiplication and tables as a means of making addition simpler and quicker. We would not want children to laboriously count out 12 times 9, or 7 times 8, as repeated addition when there are instant ways of achieving a result.

Similarly, when is a problem a subtraction or a division? We would not want children to continue to 'share' larger numbers by repeated subtraction, when division would solve the problem in a fraction of the time.

When faced with complex problems, the choice may be difficult. Consider the following problems and think how you might help a child to solve each one. In which order are the multiple operations where these apply?

a) One step problem – I have 9 sweets in my bag. I've eaten 3. How many did I have to start with?

b) Two step problem – A box contains 2 green, 2 blue and 2 red pencils. How many pencils are in 10 boxes?

c) Money problem – Dad gave Tim 30p. Aunt Ellen doubled it. Uncle Eddie added 25p. Could Tim buy a set of felt tips for £1?

d) Time problem – Helen got on the train at 9.00. The journey took one and half hours. What time did Helen leave the train?

e) Length problem – Alex's dog is 40cm tall. Kim's dog is twice as tall as Alex's. Ben's dog is 10cm taller than Alex's. Whose dog is the tallest?

Adults can help by guiding children through the order of operations. For example, problem c) requires multiplication, then addition, then subtraction from £1.

To solve problems children also need to recall relevant mathematical facts. Knowing and recalling facts such as times tables (by Year 2, children should know those for 2, 5 and 10) marks the difference between solving problems quickly and easily, rather than slowly and laboriously. Similarly, knowing the inverse facts for division (2 × 5 = 10, so 10 divided by 5 = 2) makes problem-solving a simpler process.

Doubles and halves are useful facts. Children should know all doubles of numbers, particularly 5s up to double 20, and be able to double and halve multiples of 10 up to 100. They should see doubling as the inverse of halving, and be able to combine doubling with time tables facts, such as – double 5 is 10, so double 15 must be 30 because 15 is 3 lots of 5. Knowing number facts aids efficient problem-solving!

More advanced application of number work

Throughout Year 2 children will extend their application of number using more advanced sequences and patterns, different materials and tools and taking numerical understanding at least up to 100.

Children should describe the features of shapes in more precise terms, and extend their knowledge of flat shapes to include pentagons (5-sided figures), hexagons (6-sided figures) and octagons (8-sided figures).

Pupils also use templates, pinboards, elastic bands and squared paper to develop their understanding of angles. They should know a right angle as a quarter turn and the appropriate vocabulary should be used. Ask questions: *How many sides/angles does this shape have? Are they right angles? Why or why not? Consider Figure 5.6. What are the different shapes? Which have right angles and which do not?*

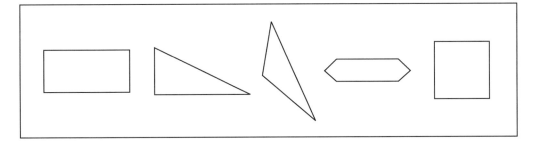

Figure 5.6 Exploring shape and space

To explore movement pupils often use a programmable robot that illustrates the concepts of turns and angles in a fun way. Children should start to know whole, half and quarter turns, recognise left and right movements and use the terms 'clockwise' and 'anti-clockwise'. They should respond to and give instructions for moving in straight lines and turning corners. They could be asked to imagine what they would see if they were standing in their classroom and made a quarter turn to the left or right or a whole turn anti-clockwise.

Measurement has moved on from cups, straws and yogurt pots to the accurate use of standard units and precise measurement using tools with labelled divisions – rulers and metre sticks to explore centimetres (cm), metres (m), kilograms (kg), grams (g), litres (l) and millilitres (ml) as precise units for measuring length, weight and capacity. Time now includes the precise units of hours, minutes and seconds.

Children will also be using data more extensively in all subjects to explore lists and tables, block graphs and pictograms as illustrated in Figure 5.7.

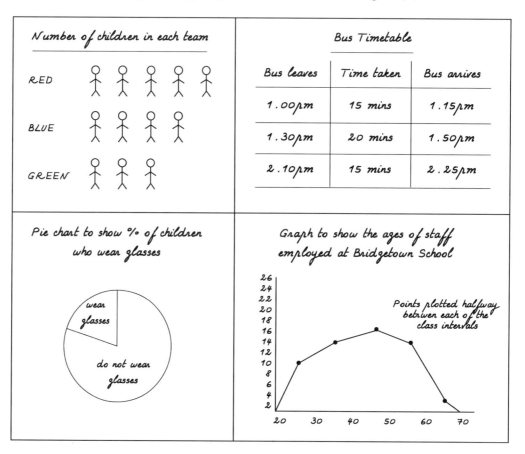

Figure 5.7   Presenting information through graphs and tables

Once children are confident with number to 100, they can use all the coins and begin to understand pounds and pence – £9.46 means £9 pounds and 46p.

Throughout all this children need only brains and scrap paper for jotting, as at Key Stage 1 mental strategies are still being taught.

Introducing fractions

The idea that whole numbers can be split into parts can be difficult for some children, especially if their understanding of numbers is still insecure. They may start by colouring in simple fractions of shapes to show how many parts the shape has been divided into. Emphasise that each part must always be equal.

Children then move on to finding $\frac{1}{2}$ or $\frac{1}{4}$ of groups of objects by sharing. Pupils need to talk about fractions. For a $\frac{1}{2}$ we might say that:

- when we split shapes and groups of objects into $\frac{1}{2}$s, there are two parts
- each part is called a $\frac{1}{2}$
- each $\frac{1}{2}$ of a shape is the same size (area) even if they each look different
- each $\frac{1}{2}$ has the same value
- when we put both $\frac{1}{2}$s together, they form a whole one, or a whole set
- two $\frac{1}{4}$s are the same as one $\frac{1}{2}$
- one $\frac{1}{4}$ is less than one $\frac{1}{2}$ ($\frac{1}{2}$ of a $\frac{1}{2}$).

Similarly, with $\frac{1}{4}$s, children should make logical statements that show understanding. From this, they start to find $\frac{1}{2}$s and $\frac{1}{4}$s of numbers. The notion that 'one' can represent a set of more than one actual number (a set of 6 is a whole set that can be split into 2 halves, each with 3) is difficult to grasp.

It is best to introduce fractions of number sets using groupings to 10 only, before building up to 100 for those children who can cope. The notion of halving and doubling has already been introduced, so the developing idea of a fraction is a logical step. Children need to associate fractions with division, through sharing.

More able children will soon start to transfer their knowledge of fractions into memorised facts – $\frac{1}{2}$ of 2 is 1, $\frac{1}{4}$ of 20 is 5 – and will be able to recall these for problem-solving. Once the notion of a simple fraction is grasped, $\frac{1}{2}$ or $\frac{1}{4}$ of 20, 40, 80 or 100 can be introduced for more able groups.

Activities for developing simple fractions include:

- colouring in fractions of shapes
- talking about the attributes of a 'fraction' as a whole split into equal parts
- talking about the particular attributes of $\frac{1}{2}$s and $\frac{1}{4}$s
- throwing dice and halving the number thrown. Can they all be halved? Why not?
- actively dividing objects and sets of numbers into $\frac{1}{2}$s and $\frac{1}{4}$s.

A sticking point, for those children who continue to struggle with fractions, is that a $\frac{1}{4}$ is less than a $\frac{1}{2}$ and vice versa. A $\frac{1}{4}$ is bound to be less than a $\frac{1}{2}$ of the same whole as there are more parts, and therefore each will be smaller. Children who have not understood often associate a $\frac{1}{4}$ with 4, and a $\frac{1}{2}$ with 2, and will then say that a $\frac{1}{4}$ is bigger, not having grasped the principle that the larger the number at the bottom, the smaller each part is. This concept must be understood at the simple stage of $\frac{1}{2}$s and $\frac{1}{4}$s before confusion limits further understanding.

Assessment at the end of Year 2

The following activities summarise what most children should be able to do by the end of Year 2. Some concepts may not be secure, but in Year 3 there should be opportunities to revisit them.

Number system

- Count in 100s, forwards and backwards
- count any group of objects up to 100 by grouping into 10s, 5s and 2s
- say if 17 and 56 are odd or even numbers
- continue the number sequence: 5 10 15 ___ ___ ___
- write 95 or 67 correctly, when given the number orally
- place 27, 81 and 39 in order of value
- say any number between 39 and 45
- say the number that is 10 less than 40
- estimate a sensible amount for up to 30 objects
- round 37 to the nearest 10
- break a piece of chocolate in $\frac{1}{2}$
- say what a $\frac{1}{4}$ of 12 is.

Calculations

- Provide the missing or unknown number: 13 + ___ = 39
- add 5, 3 and 10 mentally
- add 31 and 26 mentally
- state the inverse of the subtraction operation 17 − 4 = 13 (13 + 4 = 17)
- recall instantly 'number bonds to 10' (some children will recall to 20)
- state all pairs of 10 that total 100: 30 and 70, 40 and 60
- add 3 to 38, by counting on
- add 9 to 64 by adding 10 and taking away 1
- double 3, 6, 10 instantly (some children will double two-digit numbers)
- halve 10 or 16 (or 36 for some)
- show understanding of 7 × 4, and draw the repeated addition that matches it − 4 × 4 × 4 × 4 × 4 × 4 × 4
- multiply 2 × 3 or 4 × 5 correctly
- provide the missing number for 3 × ___ = 15
- recite 2 and 10 times tables (or use a number square correctly to multiply).

Measures

- Give a sensible estimate for the length of the classroom in metres
- measure objects to the nearest cm or m
- choose the correct units to measure the length of a garden fence and a pencil
- read a clock in hours, half past, quarter past and quarter to
- put the months of the year into sequence.

Shape and space

- Draw a square, rectangle, circle and triangle, and name other shapes
- design a mosaic floor using squares and/or rectangles
- fold a square or rectangle to show a line of symmetry and complete symmetrical shapes
- perform a whole, half and quarter turn
- point to some right-angled shapes in the classroom
- give simple directions using a plan: 'go straight on', 'turn right at the church', 'go to the end', 'turn left' and so on.

Using data

- Read a table of information, and make one
- read and design a block graph.

Money

- Group a set of coins to show amounts such as £8.64.

Reasoning and problem-solving

- Explain why 94 is less than 100
- explain an operation: *What do you do to find half?*
- explain their own way of solving a problem
- choose the best way to work out a problem
- answer questions: *What if . . .?* and *Why is . . .?*

Inevitably, a few children will struggle with many of the above tasks, but remember that the NNS recognises the time lapse between what is taught and what is eventually learned. The above areas of questioning should identify where intervention is needed. Many children will have extended their understanding beyond these levels. Others will be working far below. By questioning children at every opportunity we can be alerted to which children need additional support to remain on track.

Ensuring success for all

Bearing in mind the principles for success, which do you think should feature strongly throughout Key Stage 1?

- Linking facts and methods to understanding – It is clear that without the speedy recall of facts, a range of methods to choose from and thorough understanding, few of the above tasks would be achieved.
- Developing cumulative understanding – Mastery of numbers at each stage is crucial if confusions are to be avoided. Pupils must understand numbers to 20 before they can understand numbers to 100.

- Making numerical connections – The inverse operations of addition and subtraction, and multiplication and division are crucial.

- Estimating and self-checking – That 'sense' of the number system that allows us to feel confident with larger numbers and calculations.

- Having a comprehensive approach to early number skills – The importance of knowing all about numbers up to 10 (being able to read and write them, perceive each one in relation to its neighbour, place them in order and so on), and to 20, cannot be underestimated.

- Instilling confidence and motivation – As mathematics starts to get tough, and some children think 'I can't do this,' it is important to ensure success for all somehow. Confidence and motivation follow from self-perceived success.

- Including all pupils – Strategies for differentiation are part of the core planning and teaching delivery if all children are to feel included.

- Problem-solving and thinking – Reasoning and decision-making feature throughout every operation.

- Making mathematics relevant to life – Children must identify mathematics with what they see around them. Without relevance mathematics has no meaning.

- Ensuring that mathematical language is understood – As concepts become more abstract and specific they may become harder to understand.

- Using mathematics to support social and communication skills – Many of the activities suggested can be done with groups and pairs of learners.

- Developing active learners – Children need to reason, solve problems and make mathematical decisions to become active learners who challenge and ask questions.

Which principles would you focus on, or have you decided that all of them feature? Talking about mathematics will always be at the top of my list of success factors.

Cross-curricular applications in Key Stage 1

The Qualifications and Curriculum Authority has published a useful booklet on embedding mathematics across the curriculum (QCA 2004). Many natural and man-made patterns and constructions are based on spatial ideas that link mathematics to art and design. History is based on an understanding of time, and data in many forms is used to convey information. In geography, children work on orientation, direction and location. Similarly, investigative work in science uses mathematical skills. Mathematics should extend naturally into other subjects.

Differentiation and the achievement of personal best

Before exploring differentiation, we need to clarify success. In my view, success means that all children learn at the optimum rate and achieve at the maximum level according to individual potential. There will be children in any peer group who will not achieve all of the objectives first time round. A minority may never achieve according to normal expectations because their type and degree of learning difficulties limit their pace and level of learning. What matters is that personal expectations are high, yet realistic.

The DfES (2002 : 3) defines three 'waves' of teaching that are intended to promote optimum learning for all and be relevant to adults who support mathematics:

- Wave 1 – The effective inclusion of all children in a high quality . . . daily mathematics lesson (quality first teaching).

- Wave 2 – Small group intervention for children who can be expected to catch up with their peers . . . who do not have special educational needs specifically related to learning difficulties.

- Wave 3 – Specific, targeted approaches for individual children requiring SEN intervention. Provision at Wave 3 is likely to draw on specialist advice and may involve adjustment of learning objectives and teaching styles.

Wave 3 includes children for whom success needs to be measured in very small steps. Hopefully this book will help you to support children at each of these levels, although there is no space to elaborate on how to meet the particular needs of pupils at Wave 3.

Each child's 'personal best' is different. Consider the following components of teaching that enable each child to achieve personal best:

- Challenge – is this at an appropriate level?
- Learning style – how suitable is this activity for this particular learner?
- Curriculum access – have all barriers to access been removed?

The statements above should remind you of the inclusion statements outlined in Chapter 2. Firstly, learning objectives need to be at the right level of challenge. By observing children you will know those who work confidently with numbers to 100 or beyond, and those who struggle with numbers to 20, or even 10. Challenges need to suit the learner.

Think about the range of learning styles mentioned earlier, summarised as:

- Visual – through charts and diagrams
- Auditory – through the listening channel
- Touching and moving – themselves or objects
- Social – working with others in groups or pairs.

We need to include a range of activities to suit all learners.

Access is to do with removing barriers to learning opportunities. For example, language may need to be simplified for children who are learning English as an Additional Language (EAL), and key concepts explained. Children with visual impairments may need enlarged font materials. A child with physical coordination difficulties may need specially adapted resources for writing.

Tracking back for children who need reinforcement

However expertly we differentiate at Wave 1, there will always be a minority of children for whom we need to 'track back'. Maybe they need further explanation and practice to place them on track with their peers. Those children with special educational needs may need to work at a much earlier level. Figure 5.8 provides examples of how we might track back from Year 2 to address the needs of:

- children who need to revisit Year 1 objectives
- pupils who need to work at Foundation level.

It is easier to track back along the same strand of learning than to continually prepare different work. All children working on estimation at suitable levels of challenge is often more efficient than one group working on shape, another on fractions, yet another on measures. Tracking back along the same strand supports assessment for learning more efficiently. Some units are more easily accessed where they don't involve the number system, for example, shape and space. For pupils identified within Waves 2 or 3 we may need to track back regularly.

Year 2	Year 1	Foundation stage
Place value Know what each digit in a two digit number represents (i.e. 10s and units)	Place value Understand numbers to 20	Place value Understand numbers to 10
Estimate groups of numbers to 30	Estimate groups of numbers to 10	Estimate groups of numbers up to 3 or 5
Facts Know by heart the pairs of 10 that total 100	Facts Know by heart all pairs of numbers with total of 10	Facts Add practically two numbers that total 5
Know and use halving as the inverse of doubling	Understand half of a shape or a small set	Talk about half practically
Measuring Using standard units	Measuring Using uniform non-standard units	Measuring Continue with the concept and the language of measuring.
Identifying shapes around the classroom	Identifying common shapes: square, rectangle, circle, triangle	Identify fewer shapes at once, as many as the child can cope with
Fractions Finding half and quarter	Fractions Find half only to secure the concept of a fraction as 'less than one'	Fractions Secure number to 10 and the concepts of numbers before introducing any fraction
Shopping using money Working up to £10	Shopping with money Working up to 20p	Shopping with money Working up to 10p
Using the inverse principle and 'counting on' strategy to solve problems such as $67 - ? = 35$	Counting on from given number up to 20	Counting on from given numbers up to 10

Figure 5.8 Tracking back for children who need to secure learning

Activities for parents to support their children at home

If it is part of your role to liaise with parents, you can suggest mathematical activities they can do with their children at home.

Counting:

- up the stairs – How many steps (are we half way up yet)?
- candles on the cake – How many? Are they odd or even numbers?
- how many chocolates and sweets?
- sausages for tea – How many for each person? If 1 pack contains 6, how many packs do we need for 5 people?

Calculating:

- money at the shop or supermarket
- how many slices of cake? How many is $\frac{1}{2}$?
- throwing dice and multiplying the throw by 10 (or 5) to practise mental multiplication strategies.

Measurement:

- in the kitchen – weighing, measuring, timing when something is cooked
- decorating – how much paint, rolls of wallpaper, and so on
- mileage when travelling
- fuel in the car – How many litres?
- time when travelling – What time is it now? When will we get there? How many hours and minutes?

Shape and space:

- drawing shapes around the home
- constructing models using different sized boxes.

Playing games:

- playing Pairs, Dominoes, Bingo and Snap to develop flexibility with numbers, at the right level of challenge for their child. Snap cards that match 100 (such as $35 + 65$, $25 + 75$, 25×4) and don't (such as 10×3) could be made; snap is when two cards that match 100 are turned up.

Finally, parents could be shown how to work with the 100-number square on activities such as:

- finding a given number
- moving left, right, up or down, and saying what they land on (to practise number and direction)
- adding or subtracting from a given number
- finding a number 5, 10 or 20 bigger than a given number
- finding the number with, for example, 3 10s and 6 units.

CHAPTER 6

Key Stage 2

This chapter reflects the NNS objectives for Years 3 to 6 and offers advice and suggestions for helping children to achieve them.

Year 3

Some of the mathematical concepts are newly introduced, while others build onto the work from Key Stage 1. A major development is the extension of number to 1,000.

Count on and back in 10s/100s and understand three-digit numbers (378)

Using a 100-number square, activities for counting on and back should reinforce:

- odd and even numbers – by colouring in and talking about the patterns
- counting in groups of 3, 4 and 5 – colouring in the numbers landed on and talking about the patterns.

Stress the principle of not counting every number. When counting in 5s, say each number softly, then multiples of 5 loudly. Counting on should also reinforce multiples of 2, 5, 10, 50 and 100.

Activities might include:

- matching multiples, for example, of the numbers 2, 5, 10, 50 or 100. *Which numbers match? Which numbers are in more than 1 set?*

  32 65 500 760 80 782 45 800 70 95 900 750 60 954 75 250
- play 'Odd one out' – *Which number is not a multiple of 5?*
- use number fans – these are hand-held fans used to combine digits into different number values, for example, on a number fan, 0–9, the digits 3, 9 and 7 could make 973, 379, and so on.
- talk about the last digit – *What do you notice about the unit figures in multiples of 10? Do they all end in 0? What can multiples of 2 end in?*

Some multiples of 2 can also be multiples of 10, 50 and 100, and multiples of 10 may also be multiples of 50. The idea that multiples are about numbers that can be shared equally (a multiple of 10 must be divisible by 10) needs to be taught.

The 100-number square helps children to see patterns. Having coloured in the multiples, pupils will soon see that:

- multiples of 2, 5 and 10 produce columns
- multiples of 3 and 9 are diagonal
- multiples of 4 and 8 end up as a stepped pattern.

Further activities with the 100 number square include:

- reinforcing addition and subtraction – moving to the left (for subtraction) or to the right (for addition)
- adding 9 – this is easily 'seen' by moving a finger or counter 10 to the right, then 1 to the left
- puzzles such as – 'I'm thinking of a number, I subtract 4, and my answer is 15', so that children have to work backwards on the number square.

Read and write whole numbers up to 1,000 and know what each digit represents

Pupils need to know that '100' means '10 lots of 10', and '1,000' means '10 lots of 100'. Talk about the value of each digit.

Points to note:

- show children what '10 lots of 100' looks like
- say three-digit numbers in words (three hundred and fifty-four) and have children write them or use a number fan
- ask children to read aloud three-digit numbers
- make the largest/smallest number with digit cards – 6, 8 and 1 could make 861 or 168
- talk about the position and value of each digit
- ask children to say numbers between a given range – for example, 574 and 349 (anywhere between 350 and 573)
- ask children to say a number, for example, 'one more than' or 'three less than' a three-digit number – *What is three less than 589?* Cross the 10s or 100s boundaries for additional challenge – *What number is 6 less than 473 or 19 less than 608?*
- practise 'more than' and 'less than' with 10s – *What is 40 more than 632?*
- position three-digit numbers in order onto a 'washing line'
- play the regular games – Bingo, Dominoes, Snap. Children like having something familiar (the same game) to help them respond to what is new (the challenge of higher numbers)
- add a digit to a two-digit number (change 52 to 524 or 152) – *How has the value changed?*
- ask pupils to add 100, take away 25 and so on, mentally
- talk about when we need to use larger numbers – paying for family holidays, buying a new TV or computer.

Extending recall of number facts

Children must now know addition and subtraction facts to 20 and recall multiples of 100, 10 and 5 that total 1,000 or 100 (for example, 400 and 600 = 1,000; 25 and 75 = 100). Being able to subtract 16 from 487 mentally and quickly relies on instant recall.

Activities include:

- stating partners to 100 or 500 (200 and 300) or 1,000 (200 and 800)

- frequent counting in multiples to aid instant recall

- throwing one or more dice – throw 'three' or 'thirteen' – *How many more to make 100, 200 or 1000?*

- finding the odd one out from a set such as – 25, 35, 75, 80, 20 – 35 is the odd one out because the others (25 + 75 and 80 + 20) pair up to 100.

Extending fractions knowledge

Children must understand that:

- fractions are parts of a whole shape or set – a whole shared into five parts has five $\frac{1}{5}$s

- a simple fraction has a value of less than one

- a whole number can be split into an infinite number of parts

- the whole number can be reconstructed from its parts

- fractions are related to multiplication and division – to find $\frac{2}{3}$ we divide by 3 then multiply by 2

- different fractions can represent the same value (equivalent): $\frac{1}{2} = \frac{2}{4} = \frac{4}{8} = \frac{9}{18} = \frac{20}{40} = \frac{50}{100} = \frac{35}{70}$

- fractions have sequential values. *Which fraction is the largest:* $\frac{1}{2}$, $\frac{1}{4}$, $\frac{5}{6}$, $\frac{3}{8}$, $\frac{7}{12}$? To find out you need to find a common denominator for each of the fractions (in this case 24) as each of the denominators (bottom part) will divide into 24. Divide each denominator into the common denominator, then increase the multiple (top part) by the same amount. As each fraction is changed into twenty-fourths we can see which is the largest:

  $\frac{1}{2} = \frac{12}{24}$, $\frac{1}{4} = \frac{6}{24}$, $\frac{5}{6} = \frac{20}{24}$, $\frac{3}{8} = \frac{9}{24}$, $\frac{7}{12} = \frac{14}{24}$,

  so $\frac{5}{6}$ has the largest value.

- we can find fractions of any number set: $\frac{1}{4}$ of 12, $\frac{3}{5}$ of 60 – but some numbers can be divided up more easily than others

- the denominator (bottom part) determines how many parts the whole has been divided into – $\frac{1}{4}$ is 1 part out of 4, $\frac{1}{12}$ is 1 part out of 12

- the larger the denominator, the more parts there are

- the larger the denominator, the smaller the value: $\frac{1}{2}$ is larger than $\frac{1}{9}$.

Once children start to work with equivalent fractions they soon reason that neither $\frac{1}{2}$, $\frac{1}{4}$ or $\frac{3}{8}$ can be larger than $\frac{5}{6}$ or $\frac{7}{12}$ because they are all one half or less whereas $\frac{5}{6}$ and $\frac{7}{12}$ are each more than half. These are the quick-thinking connections that children need to make to solve fraction problems. Activities to insert missing values such as those below will help children to reason at different levels of challenge.

Simple: $\frac{1}{2}$ $\frac{1}{3}$ $\frac{1}{4}$ ___ $\frac{1}{6}$ ___ $\frac{1}{8}$ $\frac{1}{9}$ ___

Small challenge: $\frac{1}{2}$ $\frac{2}{4}$ $\frac{3}{6}$ ___ ___ $\frac{6}{12}$ ___ ___

Medium challenge: $\frac{1}{4}$ ___ $\frac{1}{2}$ ___ $\frac{3}{4}$ ___ 1

More challenge: ___ $\frac{1}{6}$ ___ $\frac{1}{3}$ ___ $\frac{1}{2}$ ___ $\frac{2}{3}$ ___ $\frac{5}{6}$.

The fraction puzzles shown in Figure 6.1 will also help to develop reasoning skills.

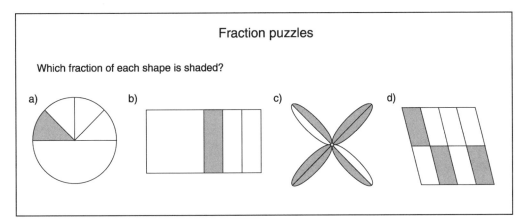

Figure 6.1   Fraction puzzles

Understanding multiplication and division

Pupils need to secure their knowledge that:

- multiplication is repeated addition; 3×5 is the same as $5 + 5 + 5$

- multiplication can be done in any order; 3×8 is the same as 8×3

- division is repeated subtraction or sharing; but instead of sharing a number many times, division allows us to share large numbers more efficiently

- division is the inverse of multiplication; $3 \times 5 = 15$ is the inverse of $15 \div 3 = 5$, and $15 \div 5 = 3$

- halving is the inverse of doubling (half of 16 is 8, and double 8 is 16)

- halving means division by 2, while doubling means multiplication by 2

- we can double or halve any number using known facts: if double 3 is 6, then double 9 must be 18 (using 3 times tables facts)

- to multiply by 10 or 100, we move digits one or two places to the left ($10 \times 5 = 50$, $36 \times 100 = 3{,}600$)

- having multiplied by 10 or 100, the answer will always have the corresponding number of noughts on the end (100×7 becomes 700)

- division may leave remainders: $14 \div 3 = 4$ with 2 left over
- remainders are often rounded up or down to make answers sensible (we need 4 coaches for the school trip, not 3 and half!).

Activities to develop conceptual connections include:

- talking about mathematical relationships
- using apparatus to prove rules and connections – if pupils 'see', and move arrays of objects around, to show that 5×2 is the same as 2×5, they can make the conceptual leap that 13×46 must have the same value as 46×13, as this rule applies to all numbers.

Recalling multiplication and division facts

Mathematical facts must never be learned by rote in isolation from the understanding that gives them meaning. Knowing the times tables is no use unless we can decide when and how to use them. By the end of Year 3 children should start to recall:

- division facts linked to the 2, 5 and 10 times tables
- doubles of every whole number to 20
- doubles of multiples of 5 up to 100, 35×2, and so on
- halves of numbers within the ranges above.

They should also have started to learn the 3 and 4 times tables. Colouring in the 100-number square is a visual means of reinforcing tables. Most activities should be short, mental and frequent to sharpen mental agility.

Checking calculations, and using pencil and paper methods

Written methods should never completely take over from mental calculations. Children should be able to use column methods to calculate, check and explain mathematical calculations, with jottings as memory aids, but these should only be used when mental methods alone are insufficient. Children should also check their calculations using inverse principles.

In order to use written calculations, children must:

- know place value – 100s, 10s and units
- count up confidently through multiples of 100s, 10s and units
- separate numbers for decomposition (by placing a set of 10 with the units), for example, 96 into 80 and 16 or 45 into 30 and 15.

Which method for addition and subtraction do you find easiest? Much depends on the numbers involved in the calculation. Flexibility is important. Children must be given choices, and be allowed to develop all of the methods according to their own learning style. Each method must be accompanied by understanding.

Addition – two choices of method

a) Adding the most significant digit first	b) Counting on in multiples of 100, 10, 1
27 236 + 42 + 65 --- --- 60 200 9 90 --- 11 69 --- 301	67 + 29 67 + 20 = 87 87 + 9 = 96
36 396 + 94 + 126 --- --- 120 400 10 110 --- 12 130 --- 522	84 + 37 84 + 30 = 114 114 + 7 = 121
76 495 + 69 + 341 --- --- 130 700 15 130 --- 6 145 --- 836	65 + 43 65 + 40 = 105 105 + 3 = 108

Subtraction – three choices of method

a) Count up from the smaller to the larger number	b) Compensation – take too much, then add back	c) Decomposition
53 – 28 +2 +20 +3 ⌒ ⌒ ⌒ 28 30 50 53 = 25	84 – 57 = 84 – 60 = 24 = 24 + 3 = 27	96 80 + 16 – 37 – 30 + 7 --- ---------- 59 50 + 9
74 – 48 = 26 +2 +20 +4 ⌒ ⌒ ⌒ 48 50 70 74	96 – 37 = 96 – 40 = 56 = 56 + 3 = 59	81 70 + 11 – 56 – 50 + 6 --- ---------- 25 20 + 5

Figure 6.2 Pencil and paper methods for addition and subtraction

Applying numerical knowledge to measures

Once the number system up to 1,000 is understood, relationships between kilograms and grams, metres and centimetres and litres and millilitres can be explored through asking questions such as:

How many fractions of a litre is a 250ml glass? A 300ml glass? A 500ml glass?

Children should be able to:

- measure and compare standard units to the nearest half centimetre
- recognise relationships between standard units, for example, 1metre is 100 centimetres
- begin to use decimal notation for metres and centimetres

- estimate measurements to the nearest half unit, for example, four and a half kilograms
- recognise relationships between units of time
- read clocks and calendars.

Activities for developing measurement with larger numbers follow the same principles as those described in Chapter 5 for KS1. Children need to talk about new language in the context of measurement across the curriculum.

Developing work on shape and space

Children should be starting to describe shapes, angles and patterns. The range of shapes has developed, as has the precise mathematical language that describes them.

Children should be able to:

- draw lines of symmetry
- recognise shapes, for example, letters that have a line of symmetry. *Which of the following letters are symmetrical A, B, D, F, H, P, Z?*
- use the four compass directions for N, S, E, W
- begin to use the precise vocabulary related to position
- identify right angles in 2-D shapes
- recognise that a straight line is equivalent to two right angles
- compare other angles with a right angle.

How do you think children would describe the different angles in Figure 6.3? You can ask the children questions such as:

Which angles are larger/smaller than a right angle?
How many right angles form a complete turn?

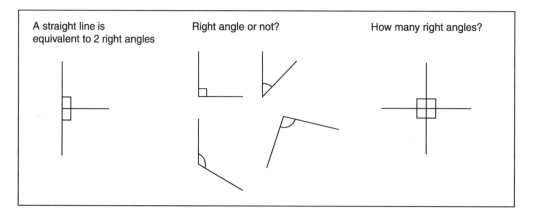

Figure 6.3 Comparing angles

Pupils should also be developing their understanding of coordinates and becoming familiar with a range of shapes. In Figure 6.4 children can be asked to describe the position of the objects and move them for example:

Where is the star?
Where is the circle?
Where is the pentagon?
How would you move the circle to E3?

In Figure 6.5 children can be asked to describe the shapes, for example:

Which shape is round?
Which shape has straight sides?
Which shape is 2-D?
Which shape is 3-D?
Which shape has right angles?
Which shape does not have right angles?

6		○				
5					△	
4	✡			⬠		
3		□				▱
2						
1						
	A	B	C	D	E	F

Figure 6.4 Using a grid to describe position

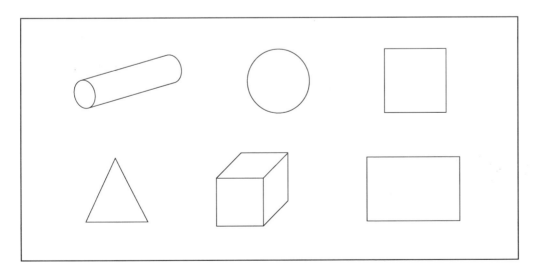

Figure 6.5 A range of shapes

Handling data

The range of data organisation and interpretation now includes frequency tables and Venn/Carroll diagrams. Working with data is not exclusively mathematical. Data handling in mathematics should support the skills needed for comprehending information across the curriculum.

Frequency table

Favourite sandwiches

FILLING	TALLY	TOTAL
Tuna	IIII III	8
Cheese	IIII IIII I	11
Chicken	IIII IIII III	13

Venn diagram – To show children who travel to school by car, or walk or both.

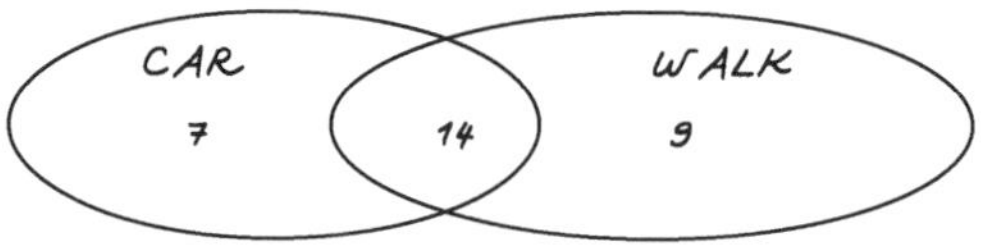

CAR 7 14 WALK 9

Venn diagram – To show children who have hot dinners, bring a packed lunch or do both

HOT DINNERS 8 6 PACKED LUNCH 9

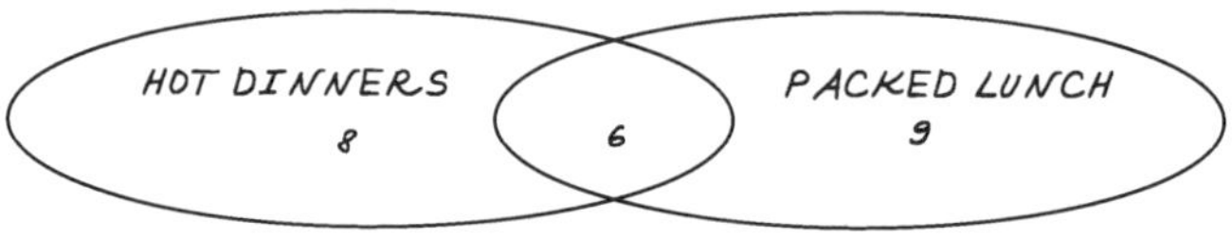

Figure 6.6   Recording data in different ways

By the end of Year 3, some children will have grasped most of the concepts taught, a substantial number will have achieved some, while a few will still struggle with most, indicating catch-up work to be done throughout Year 4.

Year 4

The following sections explore strategies for helping pupils to achieve the Year 4 objectives.

Place value, ordering and rounding

During Year 4, children need to know that:

- 1,000 is made up of 10 lots of 100 or 100 lots of 10
- the left digit has the highest value and is 'significant'.

In any four-digit number, for example 8,692, children must understand that:

- 8 means 8,000
- 6 means 600
- 9 means 90
- 2 means 2 units.

Activities for helping children to understand four-digit numbers include:

- asking children to separate each digit and write what each represents
- talking about the meaning of each digit
- using number fans to show larger and smaller numbers, for example, 5,937 could make the largest value of 9,753, the smallest of 3,579, or values between
- using number cards – children select numbers less/more than a given number
- using sets of number cards to form two four-digit numbers with a given difference, for example of 300 (7,681 and 7,381)
- reading, writing or matching four-digit numbers and words
- starting with a four-digit number children change the 1,000, 100, or 10s digit, and say how much more or less the changed number is now worth. For example, reduce 6,931 by 3,000 to 3,931, by 200 to 3,731, by 10 to 3,721 (simple); reduce 8,935 by 4,500 to 4435, by 600 to 3,835, by 40 to 3,795 (challenging). Cross the thousand or hundred barriers for greater challenge.

Children now have to count on or back in 10s, 100s and 1,000s, and to add or subtract 1, 10, 100 or 1,000 from any integer (number). They also have to multiply or divide any integer to 1,000 by 10 and 100, and understand the effect (noughts on the end): $594 \times 10 = 5,940$; $59 \times 100 = 5,900$; $3 \times 1,000 = 3,000$.

Using symbols correctly and rounding up or down

In Year 4, the codes for 'more than' (>) and 'less than' (<) are added to the repertoire, and children need to internalise these: 348 is ___ 874; 46 is ___ 23.
    Pupils should be able to round up or down to the nearest 1,000, 100, 10 or any multiple:

- 7,648 rounded to the nearest 1,000 is 8,000 (up)
- 3,476 rounded to the nearest 100 is 3,500 (up)
- 5,681 rounded to the nearest 10 is 5,680 (down).

Number sequences and multiples

Completing number sequences helps children to count in regular amounts. To complete these, children need to recognise the patterns. Are the numbers increasing or decreasing? Is the increase or decrease constant or not?

    25, 50, 75 _____ 500
    30, 60, 90, 120 _____ 480
    150, 300, 450 _____ 900

We also need to reinforce multiples, odd and even numbers and doubling and halving at this extended level.

To practise multiples children can:

- sort numbers into multiples
- find the odd one out from a set (or more challenging, from two sets).

To practise odd and even numbers, children can:

- colour in or say the times tables. They should be reminded that multiplication tables are linked to multiples: the number 6 is even so all multiples of 6 are also even. The same is not true of odd numbers, as shown by the multiples of 3: 6, 9, 12, 15, 18, 21, 24, 27, 30
- state if a given four-digit number is odd or even
- categorise numbers into odd and even, three-digit, four-digit and so on.

To double and halve, children can:

- double four-digit numbers (challenging!)
- halve four-digit numbers
- match pairs of numbers that represent doubles and halves. From a given list of numbers, children can identify pairs. For example, 40 and 80 (as a double and a half) from a list that includes 40, 6, 500, 12, 80, 450, 150, 900, 300, 250.

Developing fractions

To revisit simple fractions, children can:

- cut up shapes into $\frac{1}{3}$s or $\frac{1}{10}$s, ensuring that each part is equal
- estimate simple fractions of shapes, numbers and measures
- talk about which fraction of the same whole is larger/smaller and why
- find one part of a whole number by dividing, and talk about the relationship of fractions to division
- find fraction parts, and reconstitute them into a whole.

For multiple fractions, children can:

- match parts that make up one whole, such as $\frac{3}{7}$ and $\frac{4}{7}$, $\frac{3}{5}$ and $\frac{2}{5}$
- play the regular games (Snap, Dominoes, Bingo) with multiple fractions that make up a whole. Snap could be for multiple fractions that are more or less than half, or are two parts of the same whole
- find multiple fractions of regular shapes by dividing them into equal parts. Talk about the fraction and the shape. *If you divide a rectangle into halves from corner to corner how many angles do you have? How many different ways can you divide regular shapes into halves or quarters?* (These questions can relate fractions to symmetry.)

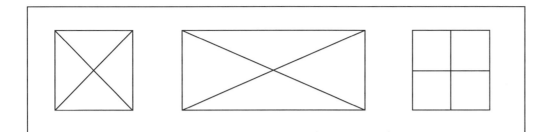

Figure 6.7 Finding fractions of regular shapes

Children need to understand that mixed numbers comprise whole numbers and their parts, and that these can be changed into fractional parts, and reconstituted. For example, $3\frac{1}{4}$ becomes 13 quarters. This can be written as $\frac{13}{4}$. Changing from mixed numbers to fractional parts (improper fractions) secures the idea that 3 thirds, 7 sevenths or 100 hundredths form a whole.

For equivalent fractions, children could do activities such as:

- matching equivalent fractions from a set of cards – $\frac{1}{2}$ to $\frac{5}{10}$; $\frac{2}{3}$ to $\frac{4}{6}$

- selecting two equivalent fractions from a range to make up one whole. This is more challenging than matching simple fractions as children have to find the common denominator to be able to pair $\frac{3}{5}$ with $\frac{4}{10}$ or $\frac{3}{4}$ with $\frac{25}{100}$

- placing equivalent fractions in order, from smallest to largest or vice versa

- completing more fraction sequences, simple or challenging: $\frac{1}{10}$, $\frac{2}{10}$, ____, ____, $\frac{5}{10}$, ____, ____, ____, ____, 1, $\frac{1}{10}$, $\frac{1}{5}$, $\frac{3}{10}$, ____, ____, ____, ____, $\frac{4}{5}$, $\frac{9}{10}$, ____

- sorting fraction cards according to criteria: less than $\frac{1}{2}$, more than $\frac{1}{2}$, more than $\frac{3}{4}$ as illustrated in Figure 6.8. Children could work in groups and talk about how they sorted them

- playing equivalent fractions Bingo in groups. Prepare Bingo cards with 4 or 6 fractions on each. The 'caller' calls out fractions for children to match equivalent values on their card, for example, $\frac{1}{3}$ called out would match with $\frac{4}{12}$ on a Bingo card.

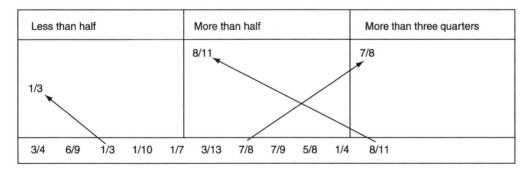

Figure 6.8 Fraction sorting

Introducing decimals

In Year 4, children start to use decimals as tenths and hundredths with money and measurement.

To practise tenths, children can:

- divide a strip into tenths, labelling each unit 0.1, 0.2, ___
- count decimal parts in order, emphasising that after 0.9 is a whole one
- talk about how many tenths in two, three or ten wholes
- divide sets of numbers into ten shares, recognising each share as a tenth: when we divide 50 by 10, each set of 5 is $\frac{1}{10}$ (0.1), two sets of 5 is $\frac{2}{10}$ (0.2) and so on
- relate decimals to simple multiples: finding $\frac{1}{10}$ (0.1) of 50, 60
- relate decimals to multiple fractions

   0.1 of 50 = 5 so 0.2 of 50 = 10, and 0.3 of 50 must be 15
- relate decimals to simple fractions (0.5 is $\frac{1}{2}$), and equivalent fractions (0.5 is also $\frac{6}{12}$)
- sequence decimals, in tenths only at first, until children are ready for further challenge
- play games to match fractions with decimals, for example, 0.5 to equivalent fractions of $\frac{1}{2}$, $\frac{5}{10}$, $\frac{4}{8}$
- play the 'pairs' game – pupils spread up to 30 decimal and fraction cards on the table face down. They take turns to upturn two cards. If they match (0.1 and $\frac{1}{10}$) that pair is claimed. The child with most pairs, when all the cards are claimed, wins
- link decimals to shape and space by dividing shapes into tenths
- link decimals to measurement by dividing lengths into tenths.

To understand hundredths, children can:

- divide numbers into hundredths; 1,000 divided by 100 = 10, so 10 is 0.01 of 1,000 (challenging!)
- count hundredths aloud (0.01, 0.02) and talk about what they mean
- relate to fractions, for example, 0.01 is $\frac{1}{100}$
- relate to measurement – talk about the metre ruler and that each centimetre is $\frac{1}{100}$ (0.01) of a metre
- sequence decimals in hundredths: 0.01, 0.09, 0.15, 0.2, 0.27, and so on
- relate decimals to money, for example, what amounts such as £23.56p mean
- relate decimals to division, for example, 5 is 0.01 of 500 (500 divided by 100)
- sort both decimals and fractions in order of value (could include tenths and hundredths) on a 'washing line' as shown in Figure 6.9 (very challenging!).

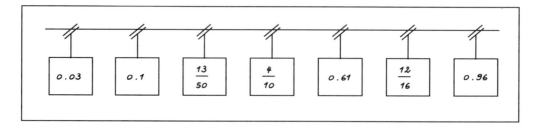

Figure 6.9 Putting decimals and fractions in order on a washing line

Developing calculations using addition and subtraction

Most children should now be using mental methods with pencil and paper as necessary.

In addition and subtraction, most should be able to:

- recall addition and subtraction facts for numbers to 20
- derive instantly number pairs that total 100
- derive pairs of multiples of 50 that total 1,000 – 750 and 250 or 150 and 850.

To practise mental methods, children can:

- find a small difference by counting on, for example from 5,987 to 6,004 (17)
- count on or back in repeated steps of 1, 10 or 100
- partition into 10s and units by adding the 10s first
- use known doubles to add 'near doubles', for example 121 + 123 must be 240 (2 times 120) + 1 + 3 = 244
- add or subtract to the nearest multiple of 10, then adjust (29 + 30 = 30 + 30 minus 1 = 59)
- use known addition pairs to add a few small numbers, for example to add 3, 4, 5 and 7, use the fact that 3 + 7 = 10, then add 4 and 5 = 19
- use known number facts to add any pair of two-digit numbers mentally. To add 57 and 63, use the fact that 50 + 60 = 110 and 7 + 3 = 10, then add 110 and 10 together to total 120.

To practise pencil and paper methods, children can:

- use column methods for addition and subtraction
- use column methods for decimal calculations
- choose one of the informal written methods (see Figure 6.10) or start to use standard addition and subtraction methods for complex operations.

See Figure 6.10 for addition methods. Children in Year 4 will be developing from methods A and B towards methods C and D as shown in this figure.

See Figure 6.11 for subtraction methods.

Children can extend addition to using decimal numbers and money, linking up the decimal points. Which method should be used to add:

- £4.23 and 98p? (compensation: add £1 and subtract 2p, to get £5.21)
- £4.61 and £3.07 and £19.00? (significant digits first, as there are only a few pence and the calculation could be done mentally, with jotting, to get £26.68)
- £69.97 and £168.84 and £204.87 (standard written, as there are no easy 10 or 100 boundaries).

The following skills, taught earlier in the NNS sequence are now essential for written methods of addition and subtraction:

- counting on through 10s and 100s boundaries

Children in Year 4 will be developing from A) and B) – towards C) and D).
Remember the informal methods from Year 3.

A) Add the most significant digit first
Add HTU's in that order
Add mentally from step 2

```
  749              309
+  56            + 293
 700              500
  90               90
  15               12
 805              602

 ex 1             ex 2
```

B) Compensation (adjusting using subtraction)
Use the tens and hundreds boundaries
Use the inverse rule to take the 'too much'
that has been added.

```
  651              746
+  69            + 184
 651              746
  70            + 200
 721              946
-  1            -  16
 720              930

 ex 1             ex 2
```

C) Standard written method applied generally
adding the least significant digit (a)
(units), ready for 'carrying' later
(b) Carry the units and multiples of 10
To the left of the column.

```
(a)  458       (b)  458
   +  76          +  76
     14            534
    120            1 1
    400
    534

   ex 1           ex 2
```

D) Adding several numbers using any of the above methods – for example, to find the totals of
254, 86, 193 and 13

1. Significant digit first   2. Compensation   3. Standard 'carrying' method

```
+ 300  (200 + 100)          254                    254
+ 230  (50 + 80, 90, 10)  + 100                  +  86
+  16  (4 + 6 + 3 + 3)    + 200                  + 193
  546                     +  13                  +  13
                            567                    546
use jottings              -  21                    2 1
                            546
```

Figure 6.10   Pencil and paper methods for addition

A) Counting up from the smaller to the larger number
From 87 to 90 = 3
From 90 to 100 = 10
From 100 to 900 = 800
From 900 to 954 = 54
Then add mentally = 867

```
  954
-  87
 867
```

B) Compensation (adjusting using the + and – inverse rule)

```
  967        967 – 200 = 767
- 189        767 + 11 = 778 (to adjust for the '11' too many added)
  778
```

C) Standard written method – decomposition by digit adjustment

```
  893    800 + 90 + 3   adjust from T to U to make U's larger   800 + 70 + 23
- 376  – 300 + 70 + 6                                         – 300 + 70 + 6
  517                                                           500 + 0 + 17
                                                                    = 517
```

Figure 6.11   Pencil and paper methods for subtraction

- recalling number bonds to 20
- partitioning 100s, 10s and units
- understanding place value.

The current emphasis on mental computation during Key Stage 1, prior to the introduction of written methods during Key Stage 2, ensures that more children move from one to the other with the necessary understanding.

Developing calculations using multiplication and division

By Year 4, the relationship between multiplication and division should be understood, and rapid recall of facts, pencil and paper methods and mental methods of calculation should be largely established.

Children should be able to:

- approximate after division; for example, 65 divided by 4 is about 16
- divide accurately and find remainders as shown in Figure 6.13
- divide a whole number of pounds to give the answer as pounds and pence, for example, £25 divided by 4 is £6.25p.

To practise fact recall, children can:

- recall the 2, 3, 4, 5 and 10 times tables
- quickly derive doubles of whole numbers up to 50, double 39 is 78
- derive doubles of multiples of 10, double 460 is 920
- know doubles of multiples of 100, double 700 is 1,400
- quickly derive corresponding halves for the above.

To practise mental calculation, children can:

- double or halve numbers from known facts, to multiply 13 by 4, double twice ($13 \times 4 = 26 \times 2$), or to multiply by 5, use the fact that 5 is half of 10

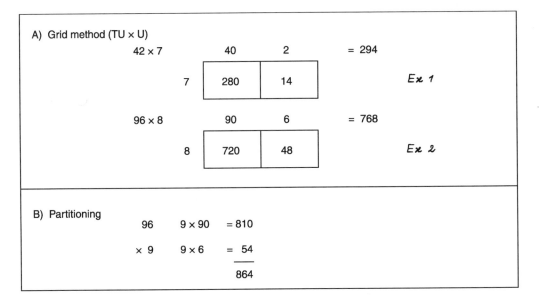

Figure 6.12   Multiplying more complex numbers

- find quarters by finding half of a half ($\frac{1}{4}$ of 48 must be $\frac{1}{2}$ of 24)
- use 10 to multiply by 9 or 11, then adjust – to multiply 24 by 11, multiply by 10 first (24 × 10 = 240), then add one more 24 = 264
- partition 10s and units, 36 × 3 = 30 × 3 plus 6 × 3 = 90 + 18 = 108
- use known number facts to multiply and divide.

To practise pencil and paper methods, children can:

- estimate first – to multiply 48 × 3 we expect an answer a bit below 150. Try group work with 'silly and sensible' estimates. Silly examples could be that 57 + 41 add up to about 1000, or that 47 is a multiple of 4. To make these sensible, children may say that 57 and 41 total just under 100 or that 48 is a multiple of 4. The statements that $\frac{4}{9}$ is just less than a half or that $\frac{1}{4}$ of 7,988 is just under 2,000 are each sensible.
- refine written methods for multiplying and dividing complex numbers, shown in Figure 6.12 and 6.13.

C) Division – using multiples of the divisor (TU divided by U)

73 ÷ 5 is (50 + 23) ÷ 5

50 ÷ 5 = 10 and 23 ÷ 5 = 4 with remainder 3

Answer = 10 + 4 remainder 3 = 14 remainder 3

Or   73 ÷ 5 is 73

$$
\begin{array}{r}
73 \\
- 50 \ (10 \times 5) \\
\hline
23 \\
- 20 \ (4 \times 5) \\
\hline
3 \text{ left over}
\end{array}
$$

Answer is 14, remainder 3

D) Standard written method (TU divided by U)

84 ÷ 3

$$
\begin{array}{r}
3\,\overline{)84} \\
- 60 \ (20 \times 3) \\
\hline
24 \\
- 24 \ (8 \times 3) \\
\hline
0
\end{array}
$$

Answer is 28

Figure 6.13 Dividing more complex numbers

Children should be starting to check mentally that their calculations are sensible using known facts and principles.

To practise division, play the 'Dice division' game in Figure 6.14. The numbers in the left four columns are easier. Those in the right four columns are

16	40	32	12	102	99	72	80
21	20	50	15	105	120	152	132
28	25	27	48	144	135	80	108
18	10	30	33	76	128	112	140
35	36	64	45	200	96	126	198

Figure 6.14 Dice division game

challenging. Use each half for different groups. To play, throw two dice. Add the numbers they show. Divide that total into each number on the grid. Where there is no remainder, cover the number with a counter. The winner is the first to have all numbers covered.

Solving number problems

Children should know whether to use mental methods or pencil and paper. Ask the children which methods they would choose to solve the following problems and which facts or principles they would use to check their answers.

- Money – Asmat saves 35p each week. How much has she saved over a year? (35p × 52 weeks: grid method of multiplication)
- Distance – The journey from Pat's home to her Nana's is 249 miles. If they go and return the same way, how many miles is it altogether? (249 × 2: multiply 250 by 2, then mentally adjust by subtracting 2)
- Weight – A packet of nuts weighs 520g. Anna eats about $\frac{1}{10}$ each day. How many grams has she eaten after 4 days? How many are left? (Divide by 10 to find the daily amount [52g], multiply by 4 for what she has eaten [208g], subtract 208 from the 520g [312g].)

Developing work on measures

Children should now be using all metric units for length, weight, capacity and time. Measuring should extend connections between:

- Fractions – knowing half, quarter and three quarters of standard units, for example, that 750g is $\frac{3}{4}$ of a kilogram
- Decimals – converting standard units, for example, kilograms to grams (1,000 grams = 1 kilogram), and representing these units using decimal notation (1kg and 400g = 1.4kg).

Children need to be able to:

- measure accurately using scales, metre sticks and simple maps
- find the perimeter and area of rectangles and other regular shapes (to find the perimeter of a rectangle, add the 4 lengths; to find the area, multiply the length by the breadth)

- read time in hours, minutes and seconds, and convert between units
- read simple timetables and be able to use a calendar.

Play mystery time games, for example, *It is between 11 o'clock and 12 o'clock. The number of minutes after 11.00 is double the number of minutes before 12.00. What is the mystery time?*

Developing work on shape and space

Children should now know most shapes and recognise different kinds of triangles. They should be developing knowledge about polygons using criteria such as the number of right angles and whether they are regular or symmetrical. Polygons are 2-D (flat) shapes with straight sides. A triangle has 3 sides, a quadrilateral 4, a pentagon 5, a hexagon 6, a heptagon 7, an octagon 8, a nonagon 9 and a decagon 10. A regular polygon has sides of equal length. The sides of an irregular polygon are different lengths.

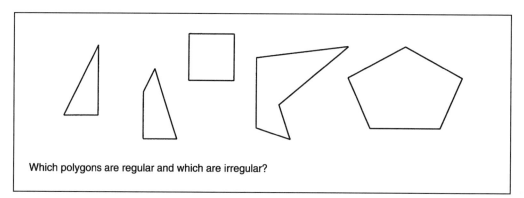

Which polygons are regular and which are irregular?

Figure 6.15 Regular and irregular polygons

Children should now recognise points on a grid, understand that turns are measured in degrees and understand more about different types of angles.
Activities could include:

- making shapes on a pin board
- talking about the shapes made, and their lines of symmetry (if any)
- cutting and folding paper to make 3-D shapes as shown in Figure 6.16
- sketching reflections of shapes
- drawing triangles as shown in Figure 6.17
- identifying positions of objects on a simple grid
- making clockwise and anti-clockwise turns, using shapes, clocks and themselves
- using the 8 compass directions N, S, E, W, NE, NW, SE, SW – points in the classroom could be labelled and children could play games that direct them to a 'compass point'
- measuring angles in degrees – angles are equal when two lines cross and when a line crosses two parallel lines
- placing angles in order of size.

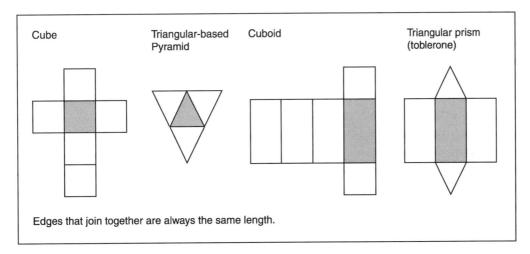

Figure 6.16 Cutting and folding to make 3-D shapes

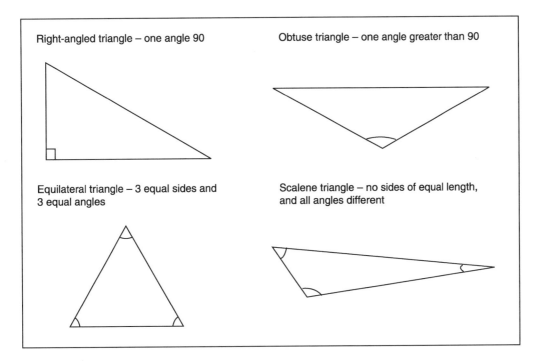

Figure 6.17 Triangles

Developing work on data handling

Children should now be interpreting a further range of data that includes bar charts, different graphs, tally charts, pie charts and Venn diagrams. Some children find it difficult to extract and present information in different ways and will need practice in responding to the range of data-handling tasks demanded across the curriculum.

Assessment at the end of Year 4

The following examples exemplify what some children will be able to do by the end of Year 4.

In numbers and the number system:

● write any number up to 10,000

- state the value of the 9 and the 6 in 9,562
- subtract 100 from 8,793 mentally
- multiply 56 by 100 mentally and say why there are two noughts on the end
- write some numbers between 5,693 and 7,641
- use 'less than' and 'more than' signs (4,583 __ 8,943)
- sequence a range of numbers up to four digits
- round 563 to the nearest 10 (560)
- recognise minus three (−3) on a temperature scale as below freezing point
- count in steps of 25 up to 500
- say if numbers are odd and even, and whether or not the multiples of odd numbers are always odd (and explain why not)
- recognise 325 as a multiple of 5, and 780 as a multiple of 10 and 5.

In fractions and decimals:

- find $\frac{2}{5}$ of a shape or amount
- place fractions in order of value – $\frac{1}{4}$, $\frac{1}{2}$, $\frac{5}{8}$, $\frac{9}{10}$
- identify multiple fractions of shapes – $\frac{2}{3}$ of a square or $\frac{7}{8}$ of a rectangle
- convert £5.93 to pence (593p)
- match decimals to fractions – 0.2 to $\frac{2}{10}$, or 0.09 to $\frac{9}{100}$
- make an array of plastic shapes to show understanding of mixed numbers such as $5\frac{3}{4}$.

In calculations:

- recall addition number facts to 20 (13 + 7, 12 + 8)
- convert 4,563−321 = 4,242 into an addition (321 + 4,242 = 4,563)
- state pairs of numbers to 100 (for example, 45 and 55, 87 and 13)
- state the number pairs for multiples of 50 up to 1,000 (for example, 350 and 650)
- find the difference between 5,683 and 6,001 by counting on mentally
- mentally add 45 and 82 by partitioning (40 + 80 and 5 + 2)
- add 153 and 152 using the 'near double' strategy (150 × 2, then add 3 and 2 = 305)
- add 3, 6, 7 and 2 in a matter of seconds
- use column addition to add 346 and 968
- divide 567 by 5, and state the remainder (113, remainder 2)
- divide £35 by 10 and write in decimal form (£3.50p)
- recall instantly 7 times 3 or 9 times 5 (or locate on multiplication square)
- double two-digit numbers
- double any multiple of 10 quickly

- find half of 4,800 mentally
- multiply 14 by 9 quickly, using the 'adjusting' method (14 × 10 = 140, then subtract 14 = 126)
- use partitioning to multiply 34 × 5 (30 × 5, then 4 × 5).

In reasoning and solving problems:

- choose suitable methods to solve problems
- explain the reason for a particular method.

In measurement, shape and space:

- measure the length of the school play area
- measure small items (for example, pencil, rubber)
- convert 650 centimetres to metres (6.5 metres)
- measure $\frac{3}{4}$ of a kilogram
- work out the perimeter and area of a rectangle measuring 5cm by 6cm (perimeter 22cm, area 30cm squared)
- use a stop watch to measure how long it takes to run round the gym
- calculate the time between 7.56 and 8.04
- read a simple bus timetable
- label a range of triangles and talk about their differences
- identify the line symmetry of different shapes
- use a pin board to make different polygons and talk about the different shapes within each
- identify a right angle as a quarter turn and as 90 degrees
- say if angles are more or less than a right angle.

In data handling:

- read and talk about information on a Venn diagram
- devise a tally chart to record the colours of cars passing the school.

Key principles that feature in Years 3 and 4

The following principles deserve a reminder:

- ensuring mathematical language is understood
- making numerical connections.

Using and applying mathematics has always been essential to understanding, now more than ever. Problem-solving, reasoning and decision-making need to feature strongly if as many children as possible are to keep pace with the mathematical teaching and learning programme.

Investigation and detective work contribute to the reasoning skills that we have been promoting. These activities can help:

- Guess the number

  It can be divided by 5 and 6. It is less than 100 but more than 50. It contains the digit 9. The mystery number is?

- Guess the amount

  It is more than £1, but less than £3. It is made from 6 of the same silver coins. The mystery amount is?

Differentiation in Years 3 and 4

Chapter 5 identified three components of differentiation:

- access to the curriculum
- suitable challenges
- diversity of learning style.

These need to apply at each stage of the teaching process if as many children as possible are to achieve the expected levels.

Tracking back from Year 3 and Year 4 work

Figure 6.18 provides some examples of tracking back for children who need to revisit earlier levels of learning.

Topic	Year 4	Year 3	Year 2
Sequencing numbers	Up to 10,000	Up to 1000	Up to 100
Place value	Up to 4 digits	Up to 3 digits	Up to 2 digits
Multiplication	Of a 3-digit number by a single digit	Of a 2-digit number by a single digit	Numbers up to 20, understood as an array
Fractions	Matching equivalent values (1/4, 2/8, 3/12)	Finding multiple fractions of a whole (3/5 of 60)	Finding a simple fraction (1/5 of 20)
Decimals	Finding hundredths of numbers up to 1000	Finding tenths of numbers up to 100	Match tenths in decimals to tenths as fractions visually
Measuring the perimeter of rectangles	Using centimetres and millimetres as necessary	Same activity, using only centimetres	Same activity using centimetres only, and focusing on accurate use of standard units.
Making shapes using a pin board	Making different polygons, of multi shapes	Making single shapes and consolidating the names of these	Same activity with fewer shapes, in order to reinforce knowledge of these
Solving problems mentally; focusing on addition of more than two numbers	Adding 3 or 4 two-digit numbers (35, 49, 71), crossing the tens and hundreds boundaries	Adding 2 or 3 two digit numbers, but not crossing the tens or hundreds boundaries (12, 34, 43)	Add up to 3 small numbers, within range 1 to 20 (4, 15 and 9)

Figure 6.18 Tracking back from Year 4 to Year 2

The examples offer ideas of how to support differentiation by tracking back but illustrate a possible situation only. A small minority of children may need to track back to level 1 or below.

Year 5

The following sections reflect the NNS objectives for Year 5, and offer suggestions and activities for helping pupils to achieve them.

Numbers and the number system to 10,000

It's all about place value. As numbers increase in complexity, ensure children know what each digit represents. What is the value of 9 in 9,858? What is the value of 5 in 3,975? Recycle earlier activities at four-digit level.

Multiplying and dividing positive integers

Children need to separate each digit and explain its value. Pupils who have understood place value will perceive 'hidden noughts' behind significant digits and understand the effects of multiplying and dividing an integer by 10 or 100, for example, 3,456 divided by 10 = 345.6, and 3,456 divided by 100 = 34.56.
   Extend activities already suggested, for example:

- compare and order numbers
- use number fans or digit cards to make up four-digit numbers
- state numbers that are larger or smaller than a given number
- place numbers in order of size or in sets according to given criteria, such as the set of values less than 5,000 or the set of values between 5,000 and 7,500
- round a number to its nearest 10, 100 or 1,000: 2,725 rounded to the nearest 100 is 2,700 (down) and to the nearest 1,000 is 3,000 (up)
- relate integers to fractions by finding an approximate fraction of a four-digit number: $\frac{1}{3}$ of 8,984 is a bit less than 3,000.

Ordering positive and negative numbers

We could think of negative numbers as being overdrawn at the bank. If I have £100 in my account and spend £150, I then owe the bank £50 (100–150 = –50). Remind children that the zero counts when jumping along a number line. Numbers below zero are negative. Those above are positive. –5 –4 –3 –2 –1 0 1 2 3 4 5.
   Along the number line shown, jump right to add and left to subtract, for example: – 3 + 4 = 1, 4–9 = – 5, – 2 –1 = –3.

Properties of numbers and number sequences

Children should be starting to understand the effects of addition, subtraction, multiplication and division upon different numbers.
   Activities for working with number properties and sequences include:

- counting on and back in equal steps – in 25s up to 1,000, or in 50s
- completing sequences that now include negative numbers, for example:
  −100 −75 −50 ___ 0 25 ___ ___ 100
- making statements about odd or even numbers and sorting into 'true', 'false' or 'either' categories, for example, X is always divisible by 2, Y can be a multiple of 5, Z is an odd number multiplied by itself, Q is a prime number
- recognising multiples of numbers, 75 is a multiple of 3, 5, 15 and 25
- investigating patterns by colouring multiples on a 100-number square
- drawing squares of numbers up to 10 × 10, to show their square shape
- finding pairs of factors of numbers up to 100. A factor is a number that divides exactly into another. Apart from 1, the factor pairs of 6 are 2 and 3. The factor pairs of 24 are 2 and 12, 3 and 8, 4 and 6.

Children should be able to make lots of statements about four-digit numbers. Consider the number 9,460. Children may say that:

It is a four-digit number
Rounded to the nearest 100, it is 9,500
It is nearly 500 more than 9,000
Half of 9,460 is 4,730
It is an even number
It is divisible by 2
The numbers 4, 10 and 20 are all factors of 9,460
It is divisible by 10 and 100
It is 540 less than 10,000
9,460 divided by 100 is 94.60
0.1 of 9,460 is 946.

Clearly, some comments will be more perceptive and demonstrate greater depth of thought than others. The responses offer opportunities for adults to note misunderstandings.

Fractions, decimals and percentages

In Year 5, work on fractions and decimals is extended and linked to percentages. Work might include:

- use of the correct fraction terminology, numerator (top part of fraction) and denominator (bottom part)
- changing mixed numbers to improper fractions and vice versa – for example, $4\frac{1}{2}$ can be changed to $\frac{9}{2}$, or $\frac{25}{8}$ can be changed into $3\frac{1}{8}$
- reinforcement of equivalent fractions. Children need to spot the patterns:
  ○ equal to $\frac{1}{5}$, $\frac{2}{10}$, $\frac{3}{15}$, $\frac{4}{20}$, denominator five times the numerator.
  ○ equal to $\frac{3}{5}$, $\frac{6}{10}$, $\frac{12}{20}$, numerator multiplied by 2.
- ordering fractions and mixed numbers, $\frac{1}{2}$, $\frac{7}{10}$, $2\frac{3}{4}$
- relating fractions to multiplication and division, for example, finding $\frac{3}{4}$ of 8 by dividing by 4 and multiplying by 3 (6)
- children could draw diagrams to show equivalents as shown in Figure 6.19.

Diagram	Mixed number	Improper fraction
	$2\frac{1}{4}$	$\frac{9}{4}$
	$3\frac{2}{3}$	$\frac{11}{3}$
	$4\frac{1}{2}$	$\frac{9}{2}$

Figure 6.19   Diagrams of mixed numbers and improper fractions

Work on decimals in Year 5 includes:

- using decimal notation and understanding decimals up to 2 places (1.05)

- placing decimals in order of value, for example, 0.02, 0.19, 1.04, 1.34, 2.09

- rounding to the nearest whole number, 2.78 is rounded up to 3, but 13.2 is rounded down to 13

- relating decimals to fraction equivalents as shown in Figure 6.20.

Fractions	Decimals (in tenths and hundredths)	Percentages
¼	0.25	25%
½	0.5	50%
¾	0.75	75%
1/5	0.2	20%
2/5	0.4	40%
1/10	0.1	10%
7/10	0.7	70%
1½	1.5	150%

Figure 6.20   Relating fractions to decimals and percentages

Getting children to place decimals in order will soon identify those who have understood. Asking them to insert other decimals into the correct space develops the notion of looking first at the whole number, then the tenths, next the hundredths.

Work on percentages in Year 5 will include:

- understanding percentages as a number of parts in 100

- finding simple percentages of amounts, 50 per cent of £20 (£10)

- relating percentages to fractions and decimals (see Figure 6.20).

Ratio and proportion

Ratio is to do with parts in proportion. We may wish to split a quantity, for example, to mix colours of paint in parts of 1 to 2. The hairdresser uses ratio to mix shades of colour, and builders mix given parts of cement to the correct consistency.

Alternatively, amounts of money may be divided according to a given number of shares. Figure 6.21 illustrates how we might work out proportions step by step.

Quantity	Ratio needed	Total number of parts needed	One part	Shares as part of total quantity
6	1 to 2	3	2 (divide 3 into 6)	2 and 4
15	2 to 3	5	3 (divide 5 into 15)	6 to 9
24	1 to 3	4	6	6 to 18
100	3 to 7	10	10	30 to 70

Figure 6.21 Dividing quantities into parts using ratio

We could look at ratio in another way, for example, that 1 person in 10 is a vegetarian. That's 2 people in 20, 3 in 30 and so on. How many in 200?

Ratio is related to multiplication and division, as well as fractions; 2 people out of 5 equates to $\frac{2}{5}$, 2 people in every 7 equates to $\frac{2}{7}$. Use practical examples to help children to develop the concept of ratio and proportion. These include:

- mixing different shades of paint in art
- mixing different quantities of materials for a collage
- collecting statistics that illustrate the idea of fractional ratio (how many people are *really* vegetarian?)

Calculations

Working with four-digit numbers requires efficiency. Children need to decide:

- which facts to draw on from memory
- whether a calculation can be done mentally
- whether pencil and paper is needed
- whether a calculator is needed.

Using mental calculation strategies

For addition and subtraction, children should be able to:

- calculate a simple difference by counting on, for example, between 7,983 and 9,005. From 7,983 to 8,000 is 17, from 8,000 to 9,000 is 1,000, from 9,000 to 9,005 is 5. Adding each step, 17 + 1,000 + 5 = 1,022.
- partition 100s, 10s and units, to add the most significant digits first
- identify near doubles, including decimal numbers (2.5 + 2.6 = 2.5 × 2 = 5, add 0.1 to total 5.1)
- add or subtract using the nearest multiple of 10 or 100, then adjust (799 + 84 = 800 + 84, minus 1 = 883)
- add several small numbers mentally.

For multiplication and division children should be able to:

- double and halve flexibly – to multiply by 25, first multiply by 100 then divide by 4, or to find eighths, first find quarters, then halve

- use factors to support larger multiplication problems, 8 × 18 is the same as 8 × 2 × 9

- partition 100s, 10s and units, 49 × 8 = 40 × 8 plus 9 × 8 = 320 + 72 = 392

- use brackets efficiently. Brackets allow us to express a problem using a combination of addition, subtraction, multiplication and division. The calculation inside the bracket must be done first. Consider the difference between: 4 × (12 + 3) = 60 and (4 × 12) + 3 = 51.

Mathematics in Year 5 relies on a sound understanding of:

- relationships between all four operations

- place value

- connections between mathematical concepts to select efficient methods.

The difference between children who, by Year 5, are 'good' at mathematics and those who are struggling has much to do with the mental calculation strategies that enable speed and flexibility.

Pencil and paper methods

Written methods at this stage include:

- column addition and subtraction of two numbers less than 10,000 as illustrated in Figure 6.22

- addition and subtraction of decimal numbers (134.87 + 87.53)

- short multiplication as illustrated in Figure 6.23

- long multiplication as illustrated in Figure 6.24

- short division of 100s, 10s and units as illustrated in Figure 6.25.

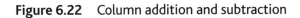

Figure 6.22 Column addition and subtraction

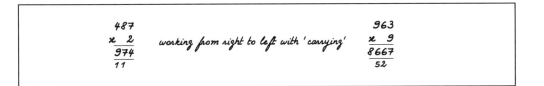

Figure 6.23 Short multiplication

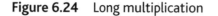

```
        89                                      196
      x  25    multiply by the tens,         x  45
      1780  ←  then the units      ────→      7840
       445                                     980
      2225                                     8820
```

Figure 6.24   Long multiplication

```
        48     remainder 2                   82 r 1
     8 │38⁶6   (small 6 'carried over')     6│49⁷3
```

Figure 6.25   Short division of 100s, 10s and units by a single digit

Recalling facts

Consider the following facts that children should know by the end of Year 5, and use some of the interactive activities suggested already to develop them.

For addition and subtraction children should know:

- knowledge of decimals that total 1 or 10 (0.2 and 0.8 or 6.45 and 3.55)
- pairs of two-digit numbers that total 100
- pairs of multiples of 50 that total 1,000.

For multiplication and division, children should know:

- multiplication facts to 10×10
- doubles of whole numbers to 100
- doubles of multiples of 10 up to 1,000 ($430 \times 2 = 860$)
- doubles of multiples of 100 up to 10,000 ($3,400 \times 2 = 6,800$)
- corresponding halves for the above.

Activities aimed at developing facts and speedy derivations need to be mainly oral. Recycle the games and matching activities suggested in earlier chapters.

Measures

Understanding of numbers to 10,000, as well as fractions, decimals and percentages are applied to measurement. Children need to:

- convert standard units – kg to g, and mm to cm and m
- work with imperial units – mile, pint and gallon
- choose suitable units of measurement for practical activities
- draw and record accurate measurements using small units
- calculate the area of a rectangle by multiplying length by breadth – the area of a rectangle measuring 4m by 3m is 12 square metres
- calculate the perimeters of rectangles and other regular polygons. To find the perimeter of a rectangle with 2 sides of 10m and 2 sides of 5m the calculation

is (2 × 10m) + (2 × 5m) = 30m. To find the perimeter of a regular polygon, such as a pentagon with 5 sides of 6cm the calculation is 5 × 6cm = 30cm

- read 24-hour clock time.

Shape and space

Children need to:

- classify different types of triangles, using criteria such as equal sides, equal angles and symmetry, and label them

- draw shapes to given angles and lengths

- visualise 3-D shapes from 2-D drawings, and identify nets for an open cube

- recognise reflective symmetry in regular polygons – how the shapes can be mirrored or folded

- recognise where a shape will be after a reflection or a translation, as shown in Figure 6.26

- read and plot coordinates in the first quadrant as shown in Figure 6.27

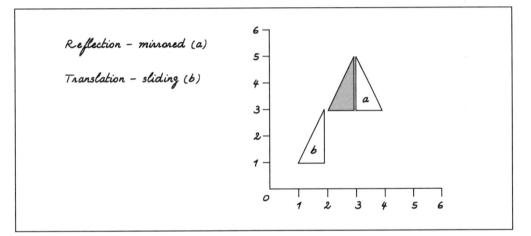

Figure 6.26   Recognising shapes after reflection and translation

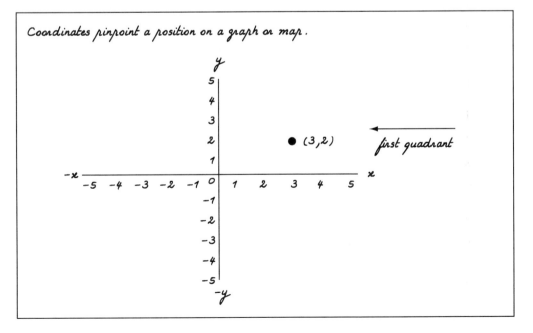

Figure 6.27   Reading and plotting coordinates in the first quadrant

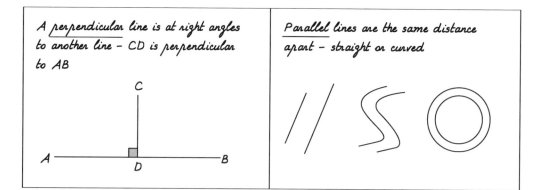

Figure 6.28 Perpendicular and parallel lines

- recognise perpendicular and parallel lines as shown in Figure 6.28
- use a protractor to measure angles.

Handling data

Children need to:

- talk about the likelihood of events – the Queen reigning for a further 25 years or a severe hurricane attacking Britain
- interpret data in tables, charts and diagrams (using ICT)
- interpret information using bar charts marked in units other than 1, and identify the significance of the information presented
- find the mode of a set of data as the most popular or frequent value. Of the set 6, 3, 5, 6, 4, the mode is 6 as it occurs most.

Data handling now extends to new dimensions and the idea of probability is introduced. Children could start by talking about the criteria for deciding the likelihood of things happening. The Queen may reign for a further 25 years, but it would be unlikely. Given the frequency of hurricanes in Britain, the odds are low.

Solving problems, checking answers and reasoning

Threaded through this book has been the role of thinking as the key to success. Memorising every mathematical fact and snippet of knowledge is useless unless we can make connections between acquired concepts.

By the end of Year 5, children should be developing their ability to:

- choose the best method to solve problems – mental, written or calculator
- explain the method chosen
- solve mathematical problems and puzzles
- investigate general statements or questions about numbers or shapes
- explain a formula or mathematical relationship – how the area of a square is found, how fractions and decimals are linked or why brackets are used
- apply all four mathematical operations to real life situations.

Mathematically able children will do all of the above, and by this stage huge gaps between the able and least able will have made back-tracking and differentiation strategies even more essential.

Year 6

Throughout Year 6 there should be many opportunities for children to secure the concepts from Year 5. The following strategies and activities reflect the NNS objectives for Year 6 as their starting point.

Numbers and the number system

For place value, ordering and rounding, children will be taught to

- multiply and divide integers by 1,000 and explain the effect
- multiply and divide decimals mentally by 10 or 100 and explain the effect
- estimate and approximate
- continue to round integers to the nearest 10, 100 or 1,000
- find the difference between a negative and a positive integer.

The above concepts are not entirely new and there should be opportunities for children to consolidate their understanding across the curriculum.

Working with larger numbers

Multiplying and dividing integers by 1,000, and decimals by 10 or 100, especially with money, is linked to environments such as banks and offices. Context-based activities can help children to think about the purposes of working with large amounts.

Activities might include:

- matching and sorting pairs of numbers that show the 'before and after' of a numerical operation, 345 and 34,500. Children could explain what has happened to the second number (multiplied or divided, and by what), and what the effect is
- playing games (Snap, Bingo, Dominoes or Pairs) to match numbers with their rounded partners, and/or sorting them. If the category is 'numbers rounded to the nearest 100', number 3,207 will pair with 3,200
- playing the 'I have' chain game orally as illustrated in Figure 6.29.
- role-play – children could be bank managers, shop assistants or customers.

Mental mathematics flourishes in quick-thinking contexts.

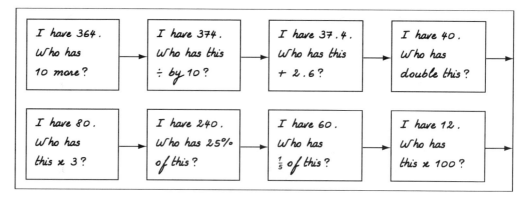

Figure 6.29 Chain game to practise a range of numerical concepts

Working with negative numbers

This is extended from Year 5. Negative numbers are best understood in context. Children may have difficulty with zero when moving between negative and positive numbers, as they may have so far regarded zero as nothing. Now zero counts! Decimal numbers can also be negative. Use sequencing activities to reinforce the notion of positive and negative numbers at a more complex level, for example:

$-25.6, -19.34, -19.05, -1, -0.01, 0, 3.4, 7.16, 7.61, 13.9$ and so on.

Properties of numbers and number sequences

These are extended throughout Year 6 to include square, triangular and prime numbers. Children should be:

- completing more complex sequences of numbers that include fractions, decimals, percentages, and negative numbers. Sequencing could be in standard units or random. How would you sequence the following values: $0.05, 20\%, \frac{1}{4}, 1.25, 2.6\%, \frac{5}{6}, 2\frac{1}{2}, 68\%$? What skills and knowledge would children need in order to complete such tasks?

- sequencing square numbers (numbers multiplied by themselves that can form a square). To 9, these are: 1, 4, 9, 16, 25, 36, 49, 64, 81.

- sequencing triangular numbers (they make a triangular shape on a pin board): 1, 3, 6, 10, 15, 21, 28, 36, 45 and so on

- continuing to make statements about odd and even numbers

- recognising prime numbers to at least 20, as numbers with only 2 factors – themselves and 1. Prime numbers below 30 are: 2, 3, 5, 7, 11, 13, 17, 19, 23 and 29. Note that number 2 is the only even prime number.

Sequencing is essential throughout the development of mathematics. Talk about the patterns of difference within sequences. For square numbers the pattern is each odd number as the difference between each square number follows the pattern of odd numbers: 3, 5, 7, 9, 11, 13, 15, 17. The next square number would be 100 (difference of 19). Triangular numbers increase by 2, 3, 4, 5, 6, 7, 8 and 9. The next triangular number would be 55 (increase of 10).

Fractions, decimals, percentages and ratio

Year 6 focuses on:

- changing mixed fractions to improper fractions and vice versa – $5\frac{3}{8}$ to $\frac{43}{8}$ or $\frac{76}{10}$ to $7\frac{6}{10}$

- recognising relationships between fractions, for example, $\frac{1}{50}$ is one tenth of $\frac{1}{5}$

- reducing a fraction to its simplest form through a common factor, $\frac{15}{20}$ can be reduced to $\frac{3}{4}$ because both 15 and 20 are divisible by 5, as the lowest common factor

- sequencing different fractions by finding a common denominator. *Which is bigger $\frac{2}{3}$ or $\frac{6}{7}$?* The common denominator is 21 (3×7). Therefore $\frac{2}{3} = \frac{14}{21}$, but $\frac{6}{7} = \frac{18}{21}$. So $\frac{6}{7}$ is the bigger fraction

- finding more complex multiple fractions of quantities

- solving more problems involving ratio and proportion

- working with mixed numbers to three decimal places as shown in Figure 6.30

- placing decimal fractions between two others – between 4.6 and 4.7, could be any decimal from 4.61 to 4.69 – each tenth is separated by ten hundredths

- converting fractions to decimals by dividing the denominator into the numerator and adding noughts, for example, $\frac{1}{7}$ as a decimal is 0.143 to three places (1,000 divided by 7)

- understanding percentages as the number of parts in every 100, and finding percentages of whole number quantities, for example, 25% of 16 = 4, 80% of 250 = 200.

Understanding decimal place value *3 decimal places represent thousandths* *2 decimal places represent hundredths.* *1 decimal place represents tenths.*	$0.001 = \dfrac{1}{1000}$ $0.02 = \dfrac{2}{100}$ $0.3 = \dfrac{3}{10}$
Ordering numbers with decimals up to three places	*smallest* ⟶ *largest* $1.004 \qquad 1.21 \qquad 1.6$ $= 1\dfrac{4}{1000} \quad = 1\dfrac{21}{100} \quad = 1\dfrac{6}{10}$
Rounding numbers with up to three decimal places to the nearest tenth	*2.636 is 2.6* *13.096 is 13.1* *27.435 is 27.4*

Figure 6.30 Understanding mixed numbers with up to three decimal places

Children must perceive fractions, decimals and percentages as related concepts and use all three efficiently to solve problems.

Calculations

The focus is on consolidation of:

- mental strategies
- pencil and paper methods
- consolidating and memorising mathematical facts.

Mental calculation strategies

The aim is to improve efficiency, using larger numbers.

For addition and subtraction, children could:

- find a difference by counting on through multiples of 10, 100, 1,000, for example, from 2,986 to 5,874 (2,888)
- use the inverse relationship between addition and subtraction
- add several numbers mentally (perhaps using jottings as memory aids).

For multiplication and division, children could:

- apply doubling and halving; to multiply 24 by 50, multiply by 100 first, then halve (1,200)
- use factors to simplify multiplication and division
- use the '9' and '11' adjustment strategies; to multiply 11 × 21, multiply 21 by 10, then add 21 (231)
- use times tables and partitioning to multiply larger numbers; 9 × 26 is the same as 9 × 20 and 9 × 6 = 180 + 54 = 234
- use the relationship between multiplication and division efficiently, and use known facts to support mental calculations.

Pencil and paper methods

Children are expected to perform the following pencil and paper procedures:

- add and subtract decimal numbers as shown in Figure 6.31
- multiply four-digit numbers by a single digit as shown in Figure 6.32
- extend written methods for long multiplication as shown in Figure 6.33
- extend written methods for short division of decimals shown in Figure 6.34.

Always keep the decimal points in line beneath each other.

$$
\begin{array}{r}
35.16 \\
+\ 24.93 \\
\hline
60.09
\end{array}
$$

$$
\begin{array}{r}
1\overset{8}{9}\overset{1}{4}.613 \\
-\ 25.5 \\
\hline
169.113
\end{array}
$$

Figure 6.31   Adding and subtracting numbers with decimals

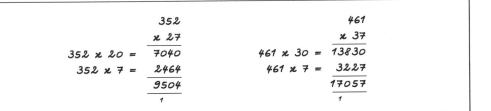

Figure 6.32 Multiplying a four-digit number by a single digit

Figure 6.33 Using written methods for long multiplication

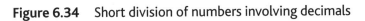

Figure 6.34 Short division of numbers involving decimals

Consolidating and extending facts

Facts that should be consolidated and extended include:

- division facts that correspond to the 10 times tables
- squares of multiples of 10 up to 100, $40 \times 40 = 160$
- doubles of two-digit numbers: double 58 is 116
- doubles of multiples of 10, up to 1,000: double 640 is 1,280
- doubles of multiples of 100 up to 1,000: double 700 is 1,400
- corresponding halves of the above.

Working out the 'noughts' stems from a secure understanding of place value.

Using a calculator

Knowing *when* a calculator is needed is the key. Even at Year 6, the calculator should never replace the brain. A calculator is a tool to support thinking and mental strategies when the problem is too complex to perform mentally.

Understanding multiplication and division

Pupils need to extend their skills in:

- using the inverse relationship between multiplication and division

- using brackets confidently and understanding their function

- dividing pounds and pence by a two-digit number.

Measures, shape and space

Year 6 consolidates and extends this work, using length, mass and capacity. An extension of measurement is to calculate the perimeter of compound shapes that can be split into rectangles.

Work on shape and space now includes:

- describing properties of solid shapes, for example, perpendicular faces or edges

- identifying different nets for a cube

- recognising where a shape will be after two translations, as shown in Figure 6.35

- drawing angles to the nearest degree

- folding paper to check that the angles of a triangle add up to 180 degrees

- measuring different angles

- recognising where a shape will be after a rotation through 90 degrees about one of its vertices, as shown in Figure 6.36.

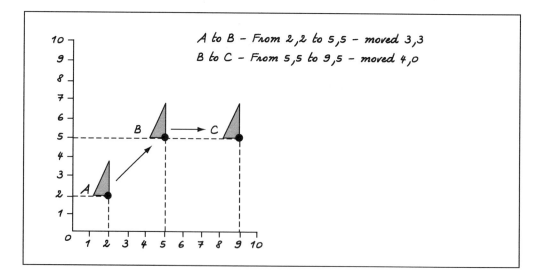

Figure 6.35 Recognising where a shape will be after two translations

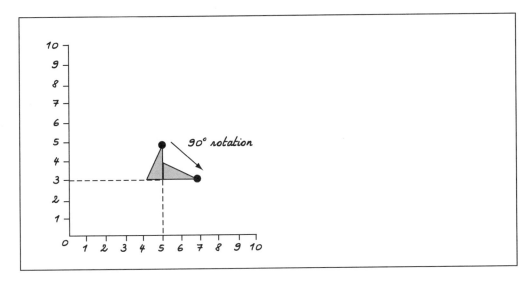

Figure 6.36 Recognising where a shape will be through a rotation of 90 degrees about one of its vertices

Handling data

Data handling has come a long way from making a simple bar chart about favourite fruits. The purposes of collecting data, its implications for decision-making and the positive and negative implications of statistics need to be thoroughly discussed.

Throughout Year 6, children will be taught to:

- use language associated with probability
- solve problems by extracting a range of data from tables, graphs and charts
- find the mode of a set of data, as the most popular or frequent value
- find the range of a set of data, as the difference between the largest and smallest, for example, the range of 2, 3, 6, 7, 10 is 8 (subtract 2 from 10)
- find the median of a set of data, as the middle value when they are placed in order, for example, the median of 2, 5, 6, 8, 9 is 6
- find the mean, by adding all scores and dividing by the number of scores, for example, the mean of 7, 8, 9, 7, 4 is 7 (total of 35 divided by 5).

Solving problems

If children have had opportunities to ask questions and reflect on the implications of mathematical activities, they should be able to:

- explain their reasoning and choice of methods
- solve a range of mathematical puzzles
- investigate mathematical statements and find examples that satisfy them
- express a relationship as a formula – x items at 10p each cost y. The ability to express mathematical relationships as formulas is preparation for the work on algebra at secondary school

- apply facts, skills and knowledge to life situations, for example, to convert English money to different currencies. Think about what skills and knowledge children need to solve such problems.

Assessment at the end of Year 6

Consider how children have developed from the Foundation Stage. Many Year 6 children will be able to:

- multiply 24.67×10 (246.7)
- divide 9,782 by 1,000 (9.782)
- find the difference between minus 4 and 7 degrees Centigrade (11 degrees)
- extend the sequence of triangular numbers, 1, 3, 6, 10, 15___ (21)
- extend the sequence of square numbers, 1, 4, 9, 16, 25 ___ (36)
- count on in steps (and back) using decimal numbers, 0.2, 0.4, 0.6 ___ ___ ___ (0.8, 1.0, 1.2)
- state the prime numbers below 30 and say why they are prime (2, 3, 5, 7, 11, 13, 17, 19, 23, 29)
- change $\frac{45}{7}$ to a mixed number ($6\frac{3}{7}$)
- place in order of value $-\frac{1}{4}, \frac{5}{7}, \frac{1}{2}, \frac{5}{6}, \frac{3}{8}$ ($\frac{1}{4}, \frac{3}{8}, \frac{1}{2}, \frac{5}{7}, \frac{5}{6}$)
- find $\frac{3}{8}$ of £64.24 (£24.09)
- solve the problem – if 1 in every 5 people under 30 smoke, out of 95 people, how many smoke? (19)
- state the range of decimal fractions between 7.52 and 7.53 (from 7.521 to 7.529 – thousandths split each hundredth)
- round 8.684 to the nearest whole number (9)
- change 1.8 to the simplest fraction form ($1\frac{8}{10}$ cancels down to $1\frac{4}{5}$)
- change $\frac{7}{12}$ into a decimal (0.583 recurring)
- find 35 per cent of 685 (239.75)
- state instantly pairs to total 1,000 (for example, 453 and 547)
- add 4,387, 934 and 5,689 using written methods (11,010)
- subtract 376 from 8,791 using written methods (8415)
- divide £25.90 by 5 (£5.18)
- derive quickly the square of 30 (900)
- double 680 (1,360)
- state the factors of 48 (1, 2, 3, 4, 6, 8, 12, 16, 24)
- multiply 73×8 by partitioning (70×8 and $3 \times 8 = 584$)
- use written methods to multiply $5,683 \times 7$ (39,781)
- use written methods to multiply $7,641 \times 32$ (244,512)
- divide 45.84 by 3 (15.28)
- convert 156mm to cm (15.6cm)

- convert 2.5kg to lbs (each kg is 2.2 lbs, so 2.5 kg = 5.5 lbs)
- calculate the perimeter of a compound shape (total length of all sides)
- sort different types of quadrilaterals (into squares, rectangles etc.)
- draw a net for a cube (when it is flattened out)
- draw the first translation of a triangle (when a shape slides to different coordinates on a grid)
- draw an angle of 50 degrees and state its type (acute – as it is less than 90°)
- estimate the approximate size of angles
- discuss the probability of an event
- discuss information from a range of graphs
- find the median (middle value of ordered numbers) and mean (total of scores divided by the number of scores) of data.

Once again, a few more able children will achieve all of the above tasks. Many within the average range of ability should achieve most of them. A small minority will struggle to achieve anything at this complex level.

Differentiation in Years 5 and 6

Once alerted to children's difficulties, we can track back and fill in gaps, but first it is important to differentiate on a general basis. Think about:

- Open/closed questions – sometimes we need to ask closed questions but by extending the range of possibilities we stimulate thought. Balance both types.
- Allow children to demonstrate what they know – time to talk could be around a given number, a shape or a piece of data, as illustrated by the examples in Figure 6.37.
- Listening to others – this reinforces mathematical understanding.
- Time to complete tasks – not finishing work is a difficult habit to break, and can erode that precious motivation that we have tried hard to sustain.
- Additional tools and materials – if children cannot remember times tables, they could be shown how to use them as a reference tool instead. Mathematical facts could be organised into a reference notebook.
- Human resources – continuous assessment should already have indicated the range of diversity and achievement, and regular staff discussions should identify the efficient deployment of all adults to address them.
- Zooming up and down the number system during the mental starters of numeracy lessons is difficult. The temptation is to aim for the middle, but with this strategy able children cannot demonstrate what they know, nor can the least able engage. Try not to allow any child to opt out for more than a minute or two. If working on equivalent fractions, include children working on simple fractions. If working with multiplication to 100, zoom down to include children who can only multiply numbers to 20, or 10.

- Consider calculators for children who understand the concepts but cannot manage a quick response, or give a question, and return later for the answer.

The statements in Figure 6.37 are examples only. Pupils will respond with more, fewer or different comments, but the implications remain. Adults need to note responses to assess learning. Such activities allow all children to experience success at their own level. Open-ended activities also allow scope for able children to excel, and to demonstrate their advanced levels of understanding.

Mathematical area	Less able children	The majority	More able children
What can you tell me about the number 45?	It has two digits. It has 4 tens and 5 ones. It is more than 10. It is less than 50.	It is 55 less than 100. It is 5 x 9. It can be divided by 5. It is 45% of 100. Divided by 10, it is 4.5. It is an odd number. It's less than half of 100.	100 times this is 4500. Multiples are 1, 3, 5 and 15. It's a rectangular and a triangular number.
A square	It has 4 sides.	It has 4 equal angles and 4 equal sides.	All 4 angles are equal, and are all 90 degrees. Cubes have square faces. Some numbers can be arranged into a square.
The fraction 2/5	It is 2 out of 5. It's a part of a whole cake when it's cut up.	It's less than ½. It's equal to 0.4. It's the same as 8/20, and 16/40. It's 40%.	2/5 of 1000 is 400. It's also 4 tenths. It's one tenth less than a half.
5685	It's a big number. It ends in 5	It's over 5000. It's an odd number. It can be divided by 5	It's 315 less than 6000. Doubled, it is 11,370. It's a bit more than half of 11,000

Figure 6.37 Demonstrating what we know at different levels

Tracking back from Year 5 and Year 6 work

Further examples for tracking back through each unit are illustrated in Figure 6.38. Remember, these are examples only. Tracking back must reflect individual needs.

Topic area	Year 6	Year 4	Year 2
Shape and space	Drawing and labelling different types of triangles to precise angles	Investigating triangles - angles and sides - drawing triangles	Finding out about triangles: which shapes are triangles and which are not.
Working with decimals	Ordering decimals to three places (5.475)	Talking about splitting a whole length into equal parts (called tenths), linking tenths to fractions	Continuing to develop number work up to 100, ensuring that the principles of dividing are secure, ready for decimal and fraction work
Problem solving, with an emphasis on reasoning skills	Working with four-digit numbers, to multiply and divide using written methods	Could reduce the task difficulty to three-digit numbers reinforcing the ideas of multiplication and division	Working with two-digit numbers; arranging them in arrays to strengthen the concept and reinforcing the range of multiplication and division vocabulary

Figure 6.38   Tracking back from Year 6 work

Supporting parents at Key Stage 2

Supporting parents becomes more difficult as mathematical language and concepts become more complex. Never be embarrassed because you don't know something. You are not alone. Whatever our level of knowledge we can support parents by:

- maintaining involvement and boosting parents' confidence
- keeping a mathematical dictionary handy for when questions are asked
- emphasising to parents the importance of instilling confidence in their child
- saying when we don't know something, but offering to find out
- informing parents of the areas of mathematics being taught
- inviting parents to ask questions – particularly if aspects of homework are not understood, or are perceived to be difficult
- responding positively to any help that parents provide, while emphasising that it is not helpful to do homework tasks for children.

Many parents may not be able to support their child themselves as the mathematical vocabulary and concepts may be beyond their capabilities, and many parents may be embarrassed to ask for help. Try to break down communication barriers. Often, once dialogue and trust are opened up and the channels of communication are clear and relaxed, strategies for support and help for their child follow.

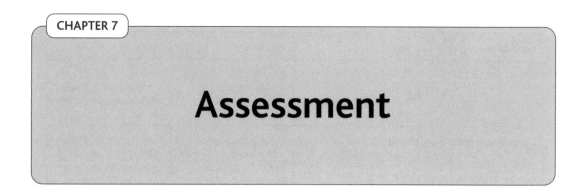

CHAPTER 7

Assessment

Why assess?

Assessment is an integral part of the plan, prepare, teach and review cycle as illustrated in Figure 7.1. Without assessment we would not know how effective teaching and support work has been. Assessment helps to ensure all learners are making progress according to individually appropriate expectations.

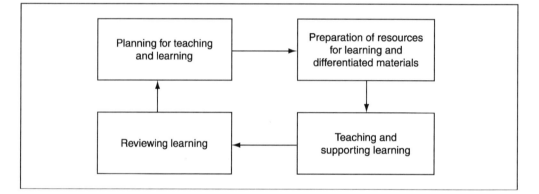

Figure 7.1 Assessment within the planning and teaching cycyle

What should we assess?

Removing Barriers to Achievement (DfES 2004a) introduced the notion of personalised learning that is intended to promote success for all children. Underpinning the personalised learning approach, the government (DfES 2004b) also emphasises the important function of assessment *for* learning.

Assessment for learning is ongoing and enables speedy intervention before initial problems escalate: its function is to promote success for all pupils.

Conversely, the purpose of assessment *of* learning is to report on progress, but because information on children's learning is often collected a term or year after the learning experience, some children may already have experienced failure. This chapter focuses on assessment *for* learning as a feature of the supporting adult role.

Assessing mathematical learning

Teaching assistants play a key role in gathering information that should:

- focus on *what* skills and knowledge children have learned (using evidence from different subject areas)
- identify pupils' learning styles to feed into planning
- include different views – from staff, parents and pupils themselves
- form part of a whole-school system of assessment for learning.

How often should adults gather information?

Chapters 4 to 6 emphasised the importance of questioning pupils at regular intervals, ready for speedy intervention. Assessment for learning takes place at different levels:

- during every lesson – it is suggested (DfEE 1999a) that adults need to 'absorb and react to children's responses' by observing groups in rotation, especially during the plenary sessions of numeracy lessons
- at frequent intervals – homework tasks, end of unit activities and occasional tests all offer useful information on which children have learned what, and what needs to be done to address the situation.

Setting measurable targets for intervention

All children are part of a class or group target-setting system. Targets need to be SMART:

- **S**imple enough for everyone to understand, including pupils
- **M**easurable – so that what has been achieved can be evaluated
- **A**chievable – at the right level of challenge for each learner
- **R**ealistic – within a reasonable timescale
- **T**imed – so that adults and pupils know when achievement is to be reviewed.

Assessment for learning and pupils with special educational needs (SEN)

In most classrooms there will be children with special educational needs who have an Individual Education Plan (IEP). A tiny minority may also have a statement of SEN. IEPs and statements contain targets and strategies for intervention that must be compatible with those for differentiated curriculum planning referred to above. For these children, assessment for learning needs to focus on both sets of targets.

Targets for IEPs represent only what is 'additional to and different from' what is provided for the majority of children. Mathematical examples could include:

- the child with dyslexia who cannot memorise times tables and needs a tables square
- the child with dyspraxia who cannot form numerals due to severe handwriting difficulties and may need to write on a computer

- the child with severe learning difficulties for whom all work needs to be tracked back, who could be working towards achieving Level 1 well into Key Stage 2
- the visually impaired child who may need enlarged font of mathematical materials.

Some children may never reach expected levels of attainment. Their differentiated planning and IEP targets will reflect their personal challenges.

General areas for mathematical improvement

The Key Stage 1 section of the Standards Report (QCA 1998) summarises areas in which Ofsted has observed a general need for improvement. These include those listed below.

Number:

- understanding of place value and the structure of two-digit numbers
- vocabulary associated with problem-solving
- subtraction – finding the numerical difference
- solving problems with more than one numerical operation
- understanding symbols for numerical operations
- strategies for estimating and checking answers.

Handling data:

- interpreting different scales on graphs.

Shape, space and measures:

- sorting polygons
- using rulers of different designs (avoiding the 'dead end' parts).

At Key Stage 2, the report concluded that children needed more support with:

- place value of larger numbers
- decimals
- strategies for working with multiples of 10 and 100
- division with remainders
- division as the inverse of multiplication
- use of calculators
- understanding statistical charts and tables.

Being aware of these should help supporting adults to focus their observations on known areas of difficulty.

Monitoring children's progress over time

Assessment data should be used to monitor children's progress over time and reduce risk of under-achievement. All pupils cannot progress at the same pace.

What matters is that progress is as good as it can be. That means knowing individuals as learners. Notes compiled by supporting adults from classroom observation need to form part of a systematic collection of data. School strategies for collecting evidence may differ, but the outcomes are the same – assessment data is used to support learning for all.

When collecting evidence focus on:

- what children have learned and secured from the relevant topic areas
- what children have failed to learn or to secure
- what catch-up strategies might be needed.

Involving children in their learning and assessment

Active learners are involved in their assessment by:

- recognising that learning takes time and is a trial-and-error process
- understanding that mistakes are part of the learning process
- listening to constructive advice and criticism on how to improve
- knowing what they are attempting to achieve (targets)
- talking about their achievement with adults or sensitively identified peers.

As part of the schools' assessment for learning policy, supporting adults enable children to be involved by:

- talking with them about their progress from the Foundation Stage onwards
- ensuring children know their targets
- showing children how to use tools to promote independent learning, for example, number lines, table squares or models that remind children of computation methods.

Assessment *for* learning enhances personalised learning and progress.

CHAPTER 8

Interactive approaches

Mathematical success depends to a large extent on whether the activities presented have been interactive enough to inspire pupils' interest and motivation.

Interactive and multi-sensory teaching

Active learners respond to interactive approaches and materials. Interactive equates with multi-sensory – we hear, see, touch, taste and smell. Research has shown that multi-sensory teaching benefits all learners by stimulating the range of sensory channels and engaging different learning styles – auditory, visual, kinaesthetic and social. An excellent book on teaching mathematics to pupils with different learning styles (Clausen-May 2005) may support readers who wish to apply the principles of diversity in greater depth.

What are multi-sensory approaches and materials?

Multi-sensory approaches and materials:

- use the range of sensory channels
- stimulate pupils' interest in learning.

When working with a given range of numbers children need to hear the numbers (auditory), say them, recognise them (visual), write them (kinaesthetic) and extend understanding through activities that demonstrate application.

When working with shapes pupils will see shapes and draw them on paper, in sand or on whiteboards using marker pens. Using pin boards gives a 'feel' to shape activities and drawing shapes in the air helps to fix them in the mind.

Multi-sensory activities also include the use of ICT. A further book in this series, *Learning ICT with Maths* (David Fulton, 2006), provides resource ideas for mathematics.

Developing listening and memory skills for mathematics

Pupils with inadequate listening skills and working memories struggle to retain many key mathematical facts that underpin successful application of the concepts and enable speedy and efficient responses. Without working memories pupils are less engaged in lessons, especially mental work. We can help memory along by:

- playing games, such as Kim's game, directed towards mathematics. Place a number of items on a table (up to 20) and give pupils a minute to memorise them. Remove one or more. Pupils have to recall which items have been removed – use number cards, fraction diagrams or shapes. Differentiate for different groups.

- giving pupils numbers to remember and write down. Start with 3 digits, then increase to 5 or 6 to challenge memory.

- play the chain game already mentioned on a regular basis. This relies on pupils having remembered the previous answer in order to work out the next link in the chain.

Use repetition to help pupils learn key facts and principles that enable success. Repetition and over-learning of the same facts in different ways encourages the automatic recall that helps to sort out potentially good mathematicians from the rest.

Basic resources for mathematics

These need to be structured, sequential and multi-sensory. A range of strategies and resources for mathematics has been suggested that can be quickly made by supporting adults, using mainly marker pens and coloured card. The following lists contain a selection of interactive resources that are not only stimulating for learners, but also illustrate how we *can* avoid worksheets!

General resources for mathematics are likely to include:

- 0 to 9 number cards in different colours (individual and group sizes)
- number fans
- selection of dice
- geoboards and elastic bands
- shapes
- 100 number squares – class, group and individual sizes
- number lines – class, group and individual sizes
- big base blocks – for place value, that enable children to 'see' units, 10s, 100s and 1000s
- a selection of the adult-made games mentioned in this book
- resources for the overhead projector – for example, clock faces, geoboards, notation signs and money
- the STILE complete mathematics set (LDA) for independent practice with a range of mathematical concepts. STILE is a valuable resource that is self-checking. Once pupils have gained confidence in using the stile tray, they can work independently as individuals or small groups.
- resources for use with the interactive whiteboard – for example, that illustrate the thinking behind addition, subtraction, multiplication and division.

Interactive, fun-based resources

The following are a selection of resources that illustrate the range available. They have been chosen to reflect a range of mediums and types of activity to cater for diversity and retain interest and motivation.

Resources for number work

Title	*Publisher*	*Description and function*	*Key Stages*	*Cost (£)*
Talk about Mathematics	LDA	Photographs to discuss sorting, shape and space and measures	Foundation and KS1	19.99
Learning Links	LDA	Colourful links for sequencing and patterns	Foundation and KS1	12.99
Arithmasticks	LDA	Useful materials that develop a range of number concepts	KS1/2	59.99
Number Shark	LDA	ICT resource with 40 games – costs from single-user to 40-user licence – a valuable resource	KS2 plus	From 58.99 to 920
Rol'n Write	LDA	Models formation of numerals	Foundation	19.99
10 Little Fingers	LDA	100 number rhymes	Foundation	14.99
Funtastic Frogs	LDA	Counting, sorting and matching	Foundation and KS1	Kit 89.99
Number Fun	LDA	Jumbo lacing and pegs set	Foundation and KS1	39.99
Numeral flip stand	Smart Kids	For counting and ordering numbers 1 to 20	KS1	4.95
Place value flip stand	Smart Kids	Allows manipulation of each digit – very useful resource	KS1/2	9.95
Foam magnetic numbers	Smart Kids	12 sets of numbers for practice with the four numerical operations	KS1/2	9.50
Magnetic number squares	Smart Kids	Matches numerals and ordinal numbers with words and arrays	Foundation and KS1	6.95
More than and less than	Smart Kids	Spiral bound flip stand to show computations as more than or 'less than' – 3 sets	KS1/2	10.50
Addition and subtraction wheel	Smart Kids	Colourful wheels with rotating spinners – fun to use	KS1	15.95 for set of 8
The Big Frog Pond	Philip and Tacey	Fun with numbers – plastic pond, lily pad seats, and range of cards	Foundation	44.99
Factor Frenzy	Philip and Tacey	Electronic, table-top mat for recall of tables	KS2	24.99
Giant, soft, numeracy cubes	Philip and Tacey	Floor size cubes – with numbers and operation symbols	KS1	124.99
Mathmat challenge	Philip and Tacey	Interactive, talking floor mat – pupils move to step onto the right answer!	KS2	26.99

Resources for fractions work

Title	Publisher	Description and function	Key Stages	Cost (£)
Visual Fractions	LDA	ICT – CD Rom for use with interactive whiteboard	KS2	Single user £45/20 users £187
Fraction lotto	LDA	Matches notation to pictures	KS2	9.99
Fraction dominoes	LDA	As above	KS2	9.99
Flip flap fractions	LDA	Plastic pizzas and pies	KS2	18.99
Pizza Party	LDA	Games with spinners	KS1/2	12.99
Fraction dice	LDA	Set of 4 dice with different fractions	KS2	2.99
Fraction, decimal and square root wheels	Smart Kids	Set of 3 wheels to practise converting fractions and decimals	KS2	11.95
Fractions tiles	Smart Kids	Set of 106 foam tiles to match into a range of wholes	KS2	11.95
Mr Numbervator's Active Equivalents	Philip and Tacey	Spinners match fractions, decimals and percentages – floor size for groups	KS2	39.99

Resources for shape, space and measures

Title	Publisher	Description and function	Key Stages	Cost (£)
Measures lotto	LDA	Bingo with measures	KS1/2	9.99
Shape lotto	LDA	Properties of 2-D shapes	KS1/2	9.99
Graphing mat – large floor size	LDA	For group work with making graphs – using common objects	Foundation and KS1	11.99
Activities for above	LDA	Ideas and activities	As above	5.99
Tangram Puzzles	LDA	Challenging shape puzzles to develop thinking	KS2	19.99

Conclusion

As stated in the introduction, this book is not simply on how to do mathematics. I've given strategies and examples for supporting the teaching and learning of mathematics at various stages, and underlined these with an explanation of the principles for success and the creation of a learning environment within which mathematical understanding can flourish. The main principles are that children need to learn key mathematical facts for speed and efficiency, make connections between mathematical concepts and develop specific language to access and describe mathematics. They also need to know that mathematics is a *thinking* activity.

I've given suggestions for differentiation with examples of tracking back for those children who learn differently and/or at a slower pace.

Now that we have considered the many factors involved in the development of mathematics from the Foundation Stage to Year 6, perhaps we should not be surprised by Ofsted's identification of the many areas that need general improvement.

At the beginning of this book I wondered if success in mathematics was the result of innate intelligence, good teaching or both. Perhaps you have now formed your own conclusions to this question. I hope this book has helped you do so.

References

Clausen-May, T. (2005) *Teaching Mathematics to Pupils with Different Learning Styles*. London: Paul Chapman.

DfEE (1999a) *The National Numeracy Strategy: Framework for Teaching Mathematics from Reception to Year 6*. London: DfEE.

DfEE (1999b) *The National Numeracy Strategy: Mathematical Vocabulary*. Sudbury: DfEE.

DfEE/QCA (1999) *The National Curriculum for Primary Teachers in England*. London: DfEE/QCA.

DfEE/QCA (2000) *Curriculum Guidance for the Foundation Stage*. London: QCA.

DfES (2002) *The National Literacy and Numeracy Strategies: Including All Children in the Literacy Hour and the Daily Mathematics Lesson: Summary of provision for special educational needs*. London: DfES.

DfES (2004a) *Removing Barriers to Achievement: The Government's Strategy for SEN*. Nottingham: DfES.

DfES (2004b) *Excellence and Enjoyment: Learning and Teaching in the Primary Years: Assessment for Learning*. Norwich: The Stationery Office.

DfES (2006) *Primary Framework for Literacy and Mathematics*. Norwich: DfES.

QCA (1998) *Ofsted Standards Report: Auditing Mathematics in Your School*. London: QCA.

QCA (2004) *Embedding Mathematics in . . . Art and Design, History, Geography, Science at Key Stage 1 and 2*. London: QCA.

Useful addresses

LDA, Abbeygate House, East Road, Cambridge CB1 1DB.

Philip and Tacey, North Way, Andover, Hants, SP10 5BA.

Smart Kids (UK) Ltd, 5 Station Road, Hungerford, Berkshire, RG17 0DY.

Index